W9-BZN-096

Knowledge Management = KM cannot be trapped in one single academic "silo" nor does it lend itself to single-minded practitioners. This is clearly demonstrated in this, Hunter's latest book *The Power of KM*. KM, in order to be successful, must follow a systems approach like, for example, the multi-track diplomacy concept, incorporating all facets of life and learning. KM's successful emergence as a powerful instrument surpasses chaos and inspires all people at any level of society to ultimately lay the foundation to a collective framework for peace. Read this book and you will be immensely enriched.

—JOHN W. McDONALD, U.S. Ambassador ret., Chairman and CEO Institute for Multi-Track Diplomacy and Christel McDonald

As an evolution biologist and futurist, I find *The Power of KM* a wonderful demonstration of conscious evolution in action, providing us a holistic strategy for implementing Knowledge Management in business, social and other institutions and organizations, as well as in our personal lives. It is about bringing much needed wisdom into our world and I love Hunter's idea of creating a globally-linked network of KM Communities as a way to address the perfect storm of crises we are facing. *The Power of KM* strikes me as an operating manual for using our heads and our hearts together in creating the future we dream of!

—Dr. ELISABET SAHTOURIS, evolution biologist & futurist, author of *Gaia's Dance: the Story of Earth & Us*

Brent Hunter's *The Power of KM* makes Knowledge Management accessible to everyone who wants to maximize the use of knowledge in their organizations. His unique strategy and tools introduce KM with a simplicity and elegance that will be easy to relate to, understand and utilize.

—DOUGLAS WEIDNER, Chairman, International Knowledge Management Institute

THE POWER OF KM

THE POWER OF
KM

HARNESSING THE EXTRAORDINARY VALUE OF KNOWLEDGE MANAGEMENT

• Business • Personal • Global

Brent N. Hunter

Spirit Rising Productions
Los Angeles, CA • San Francisco, CA

Spirit Rising Productions

Copyright © 2016 by Brent N. Hunter
All rights reserved
ISBN: 978-0-9979777-1-4
Library of Congress Control Number: 2015913924
Edition: First
Format: Paperback
Published: 8/8/16

All rights reserved.
No part of this book may be reproduced or transmitted in any form or by any means, electronic or mechanical, including photocopying, scanning, recording or by any information storage and retrieval system without the advance express permission in writing from Spirit Rising Productions.

Spirit Rising Productions
2261 Market Street, Suite 637
San Francisco, CA 94114

Visit our website at SpiritRising.TV

DEDICATION

This book is dedicated to all searchers of knowledge and to those who are searching for ways to improve business, our personal lives and/or the world at large.

OTHER BOOKS BY
BRENT N. HUNTER

The Rainbow Bridge:
Bridge to Inner Peace and to World Peace

Nuggets of Wisdom:
Quotes to Ponder and Inspire

More Nuggets of Wisdom:
Quotes to Ponder and Inspire

The Pieces of Our Puzzle:
An Integrated Approach to Personal Success
and Well-Being

CONTENTS

ACKNOWLEDGMENTS   XV

PREFACE   XXI

1. INTRODUCTION TO KM   1
   Origins of This Book   4
   Background and The Big Picture   6
   What You Will Learn   7
   What is Knowledge?   9
   The DIKW Pyramid   12
   What is Knowledge Management?   14
   KM in Action   16
   How to Read This Book   18

2. SEVEN KEY FACETS OF KM   21
   Facet 1: Assess Information / Knowledge   23
   Facet 2: Collect / Capture Knowledge   24

Facet 3: Store / Update Knowledge   25

Facet 4: Find Knowledge   26

Facet 5: Synthesize / Create New Knowledge   27

Facet 6: Leverage Knowledge   28

Facet 7: Share Knowledge   30

3. SEVEN KEY PRACTICE AREAS OF KM   **33**

Practice Area 1: On-Boarding and Off-Boarding   34

Practice Area 2: Facilitate Continuous Learning   43

Lessons Learned Meeting Ground Rules   51

Practice Area 3: Identify, Implement and Share Best Practices   53

Practice Area 4: Knowledge Repositories   56

Practice Area 5: Increase Innovation   59

Practice Area 6: Share and Collaborate   62

Practice Area 7: Measurement / Analysis   65

4. SEVEN KEY PILLARS OF KM   **69**

Foundation of Individual and Organizational Knowledge, and Organizational Change Management   72

Pillar 1: Reduce Knowledge Discovery Time   74

Pillar 2: Improve Knowledge Processes   76

Pillar 3: Foster Knowledge-Based Teamwork   77

Pillar 4: Integrate / Leverage New Knowledge   79

Pillar 5: Collaborate / Share Knowledge   80

Pillar 6: Manage Knowledge Risks   81

Pillar 7: Promote 3-Way Enterprise Knowledge   84

The Results: Increased Efficiency, Productivity and Effectiveness   86

Three Ways to Use the Seven Key Pillars of KM   86

5. SEVEN KEY LENSES OF KM   **91**

Lens 1: Business   92

Lens 2: Organizations and Institutions   94

Lens 3: Projects   98

Lens 4: Personal Lives   101

Lens 5: Local Communities   108

Lens 6: Global Community   109

Lens 7: Culture/Society   113

6. SEVEN STEP KM STRATEGY   **117**

Step 1: Assess Environment   119

Step 2: Survey and Facilitate Existing KM Activities   120

Step 3: Plan KM Initiatives   120

Step 4: Implement KM Initiatives   121
   Implement No-Cost & Low-Cost   121
   KM Initiatives
   Implement Larger KM Initiatives   122

Step 5: Perform Change Management   122

Step 6: Implement KM Governance   128

Step 7: Socialize, Share and Collaborate   131

7. WISDOM   **135**

8. A VISION FOR THE FUTURE OF KM   **153**

Wisdom-Infused Knowledge   153

KM Becomes Mainstream   153

Elevated Priority of Continuous Learning   154

Continuous Improvement Through   154
Best Practices and Innovation

Metrics to Ensure Success   155

Renewed Appreciation for Knowledge   155

On-Boarding, Off-Boarding, Lessons   155
Learned, Best Practices and Other KM Initiatives

Development of Powerful New Systems   156

Infusion of Wisdom into the   156
Business World

The Rise of Benefit Corporations   157

Solving Problems Using KM,   157
Conversation, Dialogue and Diplomacy

The Advent of a Globally-Connected   157
Network of KM Communities

KM Improves the Quality of Life Worldwide 158

9. CALL TO ACTION   159

The World Needs KM   159

Personal KM   160

KM in Every Organization Worldwide   160

Top-Down KM   161

Bottom-Up/Grassroots KM   162

Bridge-Building KM   163

Global Network of KM Communities   164

10. SEVEN STEP KM STRATEGY   167
EXAMPLE WALKTHROUGH

Step 1: Assess Environment   169

Step 2: Survey and Facilitate Existing   169
KM Activities

Step 3: Plan KM Initiatives   170
  Pillar 1: Reduce Knowledge Discovery Time   173
  Pillar 2: Improve Knowledge Processes   174
  Pillar 3: Foster Knowledge-Based Teamwork   176
  Pillar 4: Integrate / Leverage New Knowledge   178
  Pillar 5: Collaborate / Share Knowledge   180
  Pillar 6: Manage Knowledge Risks   181
  Pillar 7: Promote 3-Way Enterprise   183
  Knowledge

Step 4: Implement KM Initiatives   190

Step 5: Perform Change Management   190

Step 6: Implement KM Governance   191

Step 7: Socialize, Share and Collaborate   193

ABOUT THE AUTHOR   195

INDEX   199

NOTES TO MYSELF   209

ACKNOWLEDGMENTS

Writing a book requires the support of many people. First and foremost, I would like to thank my beloved wife Dea Hunter, for your tireless support and assistance while writing this book. Your love, patience and commitment to the causes of Knowledge Management and universal peace are priceless. Thank you for the blessing of your precious presence in my life.

Special thanks and appreciation go to the International Knowledge Management Institute (KMI) for the education and inspiration I've received.

I would also like to acknowledge one of the most authentic and special people I've ever known, Carmel Rivello Maguire. Thank you for your friendship and for your tireless commitment to touching the lives of so many people around you.

Thank you Wendy Boul, for your friendship and our partnership in KM at work. The thoughtfulness and love you put into everything you do are rare and precious. You are an amazing and inspiring gift to the world.

Thank you Kae Sable, "Possibilitarian." You are very inspiring and embody the essence of how to live our lives authentically in an open-ended universe where anything is possible. Thank you for our friendship and partnership with KM at work.

Thank you Christine Moore, for the outstanding assistance and guidance you provided during the editing of this book. Your brilliant feedback and suggestions were invaluable.

Thank you Mary Langford, for the excellent job you did in copyediting this book. Your attention to detail is impressive and helped make this book even more readable.

Thank you Aldo Delgado (AldoDelgado.com), for the awesome job you did in creating the artwork for the book cover, website, Powerpoint presentation and other related materials.

Thank you Susan Shankin, for the beautiful job you did in designing the inside of this book.

Thank you for your ever-present love and support, my beautiful sisters Nicole Rezan Hunter and Elise Suzanne Güner Hunter Matthews.

Thank you Wikipedia Foundation, for making it so easy to access high-quality, encyclopedic content on the web. You are already making an enormous difference in shifting the consciousness of humanity at this historic time.

Thank you to everyone who has provided interest, support and inspiration for the four editions of *The Rainbow Bridge* and the universal wisdom contained within it. As we will see in *The Power of KM*, wisdom is the apex of the DIKW Pyramid. Therefore, *The Rainbow Bridge* plays an important role in the creation of *The Power of KM*.

The following amazing people provided wonderful endorsements for *The Rainbow Bridge*: Dr. Reza Aslan, Dain Blanton, Andrew Cohen, Bill Froehlich, Dr. Arun Gandhi, Dr. Ashok Gangadean, Ron Garan,

William Gladstone, Louis Gossett, Jr., H.H. the 14th Dalai Lama Tenzin Gyatso, Hazel Henderson, Marilyn King, Dr. David Krieger, Dr. Ervin Laszlo, Ambassador John W. McDonald, Dr. Edgar Mitchell (deceased), Barbara Muller, James O'Dea, Governor and Ambassador Bill Richardson, Dr. Nancy Roof, Dr. Elisabet Sahtouris, Namira Salim, Dr. Marilyn Schlitz, Neale Donald Walsch, Dr. Brother Wayne Teasdale (deceased) and Dr. Robert Thurman.

Thank you, all former Advisors and supporters of The Park (1994-2001), the world's first intentionally global online community. Your support meant the world to me. Your commitment to the vision of a harmonious world community in cyberspace was inspiring and humbling. Similar to the way *The Rainbow Bridge* helped give rise to this book, The Park provided the experience that led to the deep wisdom contained in *The Rainbow Bridge* and thus anyone who helped support The Park was important in the creation of this book. Members of The Park's Board of Advisors and friends are as follows: Jon Appleton, Donna Attewell, Elise Bauer, Brent Britton, Tom Cervantez, Mark Comings, Richard Curtis, Troy Davis, Steven R. Desdier (deceased), Gary Wayne

Farris, John Fasano, David Field, Ron Fleisher, Jim Fournier, Helen Grieco, Cheryl Haley, Chad Hamilton, Jan Hauser, Dr. Jean Houston, Jack Hunter (deceased), Jayne Landon, Dr. Pierre Lévy, Bernard Lietaer, Bill Louden, Richard Lukens, Francis X. Maguire (deceased), Kenneth Mackler, Dr. Drew E. Maris, Barbara Marx Hubbard, Dr. Jeffrey Mishlove, Dr. Brian O'Leary (deceased), Dr. Paul H. Ray, John Renesch, Howard Rheingold, Annette Riggs, Ray Rike, Dame Anita Roddick (deceased), Peter Russell, Dr. Elisabet Sahtouris, Gil Silberman, Jan St. John, Dr. Elisabeth Targ (deceased), David Turk, Rick Weintraub, Marianne Williamson and Reinhold Ziegler.

PREFACE

I am excited to share this book with you on Knowledge Management (KM) that includes a comprehensive, integrated, holistic, universal strategy that can be infinitely customized for use in any business or organization in the world.

As you learn more about KM, you will appreciate the simplicity and elegance with which we can leverage knowledge in the world of business. You may also realize that you are already performing KM, even if you didn't know it or use the related terminology.

The chief aim of this book is to introduce the concept of KM and make it as accessible as possible to the largest number of people. The information here will allow you to leverage this profound tool in your business, personal life and even as a way to help resolve many of the world's challenges.

This book is relatively brief, so that you can get started using and witnessing the power of KM as quickly as possible. You will see the possibilities of KM's critical role in helping to bring about positive changes in our lives. By the time you finish reading this book, you will learn that knowledge is power and that KM is extraordinarily valuable.

Brent N. Hunter
West Hills, California
August 8, 2016

"In an economy where the only certainty is uncertainty, the one sure source of lasting competitive advantage is knowledge."

—IKUJIRO NONAKA
author of *The Knowledge-Creating Company*

1.

INTRODUCTION TO KM

As Sir Francis Bacon stated, "knowledge is power"—and knowledge is powerful. Knowledge enabled the Allied cryptologists to break the German enigma machine during World War II. Knowledge allowed the Mars rover *Curiosity* to touch down, drive around, take samples and send images of the surface of Mars back to Earth after a 350 million mile journey.[1] Knowledge enabled Albert Einstein and Stephen Hawking to make astonishing breakthroughs in science and physics. Knowledge has helped humankind do amazing things.

Similarly, lack of knowledge can be exceedingly costly. Just one example is the Volkswagen emission scandal,

---

1 National Aeronautics and Space Administration (NASA)

where the company was caught cheating on emissions tests in its diesel vehicles. This scandal could cost the world's largest automaker up to $86 billion, according to Credit Suisse analysts.[2] If the right people in upper management had the knowledge of what was happening, they might have been able to prevent the loss of tens of billions of dollars—the cost to fix the emissions problems, reimburse owners for the loss of value to their vehicles and to settle civil and criminal court cases. The VW scandal could be even bigger than the Enron scandal and BP Deepwater scandal combined.

The cultivation, harvesting and utilization of knowledge through the science and art of Knowledge Management (KM) is extraordinarily valuable. Well-implemented KM allows organizations and people to make better decisions that produce more effective results, with greater efficiency and productivity, often with significant cost savings, in all areas of our lives.

I've developed a unique strategy for implementing Knowledge Management that explains how you can have the following powerful tools at your disposal:

2 CNN, CNBC and CNET (October 2, 2015)

1. Seven Key Facets of KM

2. Seven Key Practice Areas of KM

3. Seven Key Pillars of KM

4. Seven Key Lenses of KM

5. Seven Step KM Strategy

The concepts in this book are guided by Miller's Law,[3] which states that the number of objects an average human can hold in working memory is seven, plus or minus two.

The field of Knowledge Management can seem challenging—but it doesn't need to be. This book clearly outlines my easy-to-use strategy and process for understanding and implementing KM that's not only applicable in the business world—but in our personal lives and as a tool to help make the world a better place.

If you follow the protocols described in this book, your organization can immediately start benefiting from the use of KM. It takes a long-term perspective and strong commitment over years to fully reap all of

---

3 Wikipedia, "The Magical Number Seven, Plus or Minus Two"

the fruits of your labor. But what magnificent fruit you will receive!

ORIGINS OF THIS BOOK

I have held a variety of different positions during my career, ranging from a software engineer experienced in ten programming languages, to Systems Analyst, Senior Project Manager, Technology Manager, and CIO/Director of IT, in addition to being the Chairman and CEO of several of my own companies starting at age 19.

After learning about the field of Knowledge Management a few years ago and moving through three levels of professional certification up to Master Certified Knowledge Manager (MCKM), I realized that Knowledge Management resonates deeply with me. I feel a professional and personal calling to work in the field of Knowledge Management and to share and apply its use worldwide.

This book is the result of integrating the existing body of KM knowledge to which I've had access so far with my own unique KM contribution.

I've been performing Knowledge Management virtually my entire professional life, despite the fact that I didn't realize it. I am now employing KM consciously and I'm dedicated to sharing this knowledge for the benefit of others.

You might already be utilizing some form of KM as well, without knowing it. Imagine the power of KM when it is implemented consciously. The simple yet sophisticated logic you will find throughout this book can bring a calming sense of order within what is often chaos in the business world.

After studying Knowledge Management, I came across a number of mostly academic books that teach the theory of KM, and a number that teach various KM techniques. However, many provided divergent information and lacked consistent definitions and approaches. I didn't find a single one that provided an easy to read introduction along with a simple strategy for implementing KM comprehensively in any organization. I realized this was an important need that I could fill—and *The Power of KM* was born.

BACKGROUND AND THE BIG PICTURE

Knowledge Management has been an established discipline since around 1990. It started with a bang and then slowed down—but is now experiencing a vital resurgence as we transition from the Information Age to the Knowledge Age.

A little historical background: civilization transitioned from the Agrarian Age (which started approximately 10,000 years ago) to the Industrial Age (which started roughly in the mid-1700's) to the Information Age (which started in the late 20th century). We are now moving from the Information Age to the Knowledge Age in the 21st century. In the Knowledge Age, we make better decisions utilizing wisdom-infused knowledge rather than just information.

The importance of this distinction and transition cannot be overstated—and this is the long-term "big picture" to always keep in mind when thinking about and implementing KM. This outlook puts everything into proper perspective and increases the probability of success of our efforts to implement KM.

WHAT YOU WILL LEARN

This book will introduce you in a powerful way to the exciting body of knowledge that is Knowledge Management. There are plenty of "rabbit holes" we have the potential to go down, where it's easy to get off track and lose sight of the big picture—which is precisely why I've written this book in the spirit of being relatively brief. However, repetition can be helpful when learning a new subject. Therefore, you will see a certain amount of intentional repetition throughout the book to reinforce and underscore key concepts.

During your journey through this book, you will receive an introduction to Knowledge Management including an understanding of the big picture as we move from the Information Age to the Knowledge Age. You will learn about the Data—Information—Knowledge—Wisdom (DIKW) Pyramid and how KM is similar to a diamond with different facets. You will learn more about KM by utilizing the **Seven Key Facets of KM**.

We'll delve into the **Seven Key Practice Areas of KM**, which provides a variety of tactical techniques and tools that help you perform KM.

You will then learn how to understand and organize KM initiatives through the **Seven Key Pillars of KM.**

Then, you will be shown how to apply KM in a focused manner—including in our personal lives and throughout society—through the **Seven Key Lenses of KM.**

After that you will understand how it all ties together through the **Seven Step KM Strategy.**

You will learn about **Wisdom** and how it relates to Knowledge Management, followed by a **KM Call to Action.** To help you understand KM even more, you will experience an **Example Walkthrough of the Seven Step KM Strategy** using a fictitious company.

You will learn how KM can be applied to any business or organization—including at the global level to solve international problems through a **globally-connected network of KM Communities** that are guided by the use of wisdom-infused KM. You will learn that KM can be very helpful in our personal, family and community lives. By the time you finish this book, you will understand the extraordinary value of KM.

WHAT IS KNOWLEDGE?

According to the International Knowledge Management Institute, **KNOWLEDGE IS UNDERSTANDING GAINED THROUGH EXPERIENCE.** Knowledge can be gained from ourselves or from others; we do not need to have a direct experience in order to gain knowledge. For example, if we see the painful results of someone putting their hand on a red-hot stove burner, we can learn from their experience and not repeat their painful mistakes.

Knowledge is divided into two categories: explicit and tacit knowledge.

Explicit knowledge is knowledge that we are aware of and can record, store in a database and share with others. It is knowledge that can be *codified*. Some examples are documents, manuals, catalogs, books, processes, procedures, formulas, checklists, training aids, videos and knowledge repositories.

Tacit knowledge is what we do not know that we know or that can't easily be explained. Essentially, it is knowledge inside people's heads, difficult to codify and store in a database. These include intuition, hunches, experiences, memories and expertise stored in the minds of people who are in an organization.

An example of tacit knowledge are the skills required to ride a bicycle. The explicit knowledge required to ride a bicycle is to get on, start pedaling and steer in the direction you want to go. The tacit knowledge is much more difficult to describe, such as how to balance your body so you don't fall off. Both types of knowledge are important. Another example is exactly how an employee performs their job, the names and contact information of people they work with in various departments, what systems they use, etc. If all of this information is just residing in someone's head and is not documented anywhere, it is tacit knowledge. Once it is documented, it is explicit.

As you can see from the picture on the following page, most organizations have much more tacit knowledge than they have explicit knowledge; explicit knowledge is the tip of the proverbial iceberg.

The more tacit knowledge can be converted into explicit knowledge, the greater the value our organization gains. Once knowledge is explicit, the more easily it can be shared with others—for their benefit as well as the organization as a whole. Converting tacit knowledge into explicit knowledge is one of the most important goals of KM.

Explicit Knowledge

Tacit Knowledge

THE DIKW PYRAMID[4]

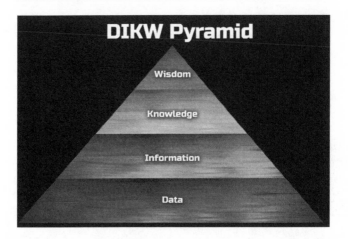

As can be seen from the pyramid above, Data is at the base of the pyramid. Above Data is Information, which is Data in context. Above Information is Knowledge, which is understanding gained through experience. Above Knowledge is Wisdom, which leads to knowing, and to better decisions and outcomes.

A pyramid is used to illustrate this hierarchy because the concepts build on one another, with elements of the lower part of the pyramid required before we can move up the pyramid. It can also be said that there are less of the higher levels, which is why the higher

---

4 The DIKW Pyramid is also known as the Wisdom Hierarchy, Knowledge Hierarchy, Wisdom Pyramid or Knowledge Pyramid.

levels occupy a smaller part of the area inside the pyramid.

This pyramid provides a context for knowledge and Knowledge Management. It will be helpful to keep this pyramid in mind as you read this book. I will also discuss this in greater detail in the Wisdom chapter.

Here is a simple example of how the difference between data, information, knowledge, and wisdom can be understood. If we found a piece of paper with "8" written on it, what does it tell us? What does "8" mean, what does it refer to? Is it just two circles on top of one another? Is it a number or is it the symbol for infinity (∞) displayed vertically? We don't know, because there is no context. It's just *data*.

If we found "8 apples" written on a piece of paper, it is clear that some context has been added. In this example, "8 apples" is information. However, it is still unclear what "8 apples" means or what to do with it; although some context has been provided, it's still limited.

If even more information is added, we might recognize "8 apples" as one ingredient in an apple pie.

The fact that it takes 8 apples to make an apple pie is knowledge.

WHAT IS KNOWLEDGE MANAGEMENT?

The concept of Knowledge Management can be understood using a variety of perspectives. But no matter how different those viewpoints are, we're still looking at the same thing. Here are a few different perspectives to consider, all of which accurately portray Knowledge Management:

1. Knowledge Management maximizes human and organizational assets by optimizing the use of wisdom-infused knowledge for the purpose of increasing efficiency, creativity and successful execution of an organization's mission.

2. Knowledge Management enhances the way that an organization can intelligently leverage human capital and intellectual assets.

3. Knowledge Management involves the process of collecting, storing, retrieving, developing, leveraging and sharing of institutional knowledge.

4. Knowledge Management also involves managing knowledge and knowledge processes.

5. Knowledge Management is roughly 70% people and culture, 20% process and 10% technology.[5] That is, KM = People + Process + Technology, in that order.

Since knowledge is understanding gained through experience, it should be clear that anything related to learning is a vital part of Knowledge Management.

KM is not about being right or wrong, or about doing things the "right way"—but rather in a *better* way. KM is about using our human capital and knowledge in a manner that solves problems and produces the best possible outcome for the largest number of people.

Well-executed Knowledge Management leads to increased efficiency, effectiveness and productivity. Through increased knowledge sharing, a natural outcome is increased teamwork and team productivity. You will often experience that the optimized use of resources results in significantly lower costs.

---

5 *Mastering Organizational Knowledge Flow: How to Make Knowledge Sharing Work,* by Frank Leistner

KM IN ACTION

Many companies are saving significant capital by using Knowledge Management. Examples you will learn about starting in Chapter 3: Seven Key Practice Areas of KM, and throughout the book, include:

1. British Petroleum (BP) saved $85 million by driving optimizations of the Lessons Learned process while performing oil rig maintenance.

2. The Royal Dutch Shell Group saved more than $200 million through online global peer networks.

3. Ford Motor Company used standard KM techniques to reduce assembly costs by $1.5 billion between 1990 and 2000.

4. Texas Instruments increased annual fabrication capacity by $1.5 billion and saved $500 million in direct investment costs.

5. Chevron reduced operating costs by $2 billion per year by managing and sharing knowledge.

6. A Harvard research project determined that hospitals across the US could save $15 to $25

billion each year by implementing a relatively simple KM technique.

7. A research study conducted by McKinsey & Company indicates that team members spend 20% of their time searching for information and knowledge. We will learn how individual companies can save more than $30 billion every year by optimizing how their people search for knowledge.

Through these examples and others, you'll see how companies can save billions of dollars by capturing knowledge via exit interviews—and learn how we can save more than $50 billion *every day* by implementing Knowledge Management at the global level. You will also learn about an exciting initiative to facilitate the exchange of knowledge to increase effectiveness and reduce costs of the world's $90 trillion investment in infrastructure at the global level.

Clearly, these are not the kind of statistics you see every day. The amount of resources that can be saved by solving problems and creating greater efficiency, productivity and effectiveness through KM is quite extraordinary and extremely valuable.

HOW TO READ THIS BOOK

It is my hope that after you read this book you will use it as a reference guide and draw upon it frequently in the future. This is why the margins are wide and why I've included the blank pages in the back of the book titled "Notes to Myself." As you read each chapter, jot down your questions, thoughts and ideas on these blank pages. The content of the book as well as your own notes will create a useful resource to help guide you on your journey through Knowledge Management.

If your organization is large and has resources to commit to KM, the full power of KM will be seen when you carefully follow the **Seven Step KM Strategy**, customizing it for use in your organization. If, however, your organization is small or lacks support for KM, you can still gain value by implementing a few KM initiatives that are found in the **Seven Key Practice Areas of KM**, and then build on your successes.

Some people believe that KM is just "common sense." However, we all know that common sense isn't always common or commonly used. By following the step-by-step approach outlined in this book, you will find KM to be simple and straight forward. If you persistently take it one step at a time and make a long-term commitment, you will be able to successfully implement KM—and reap its extraordinary value.

2.

SEVEN KEY FACETS OF KM

Appreciating and utilizing KM is similar to looking at a diamond; it looks slightly different depending on which angle you're viewing it from. As mentioned in the prior chapter, KM can be viewed from different perspectives; depending on the vantage point, KM may appear to be slightly different but it's still KM. This is true for any organization anywhere in the world.

The diagram on the next page represents a logical way to understand the various facets of KM. In many cases, KM takes place in the order shown. However, it is also possible for our KM activities to take place in a non-linear fashion. For example, if your company's R&D department creates new knowledge (Step 5), such as a developing a new medical treatment, that

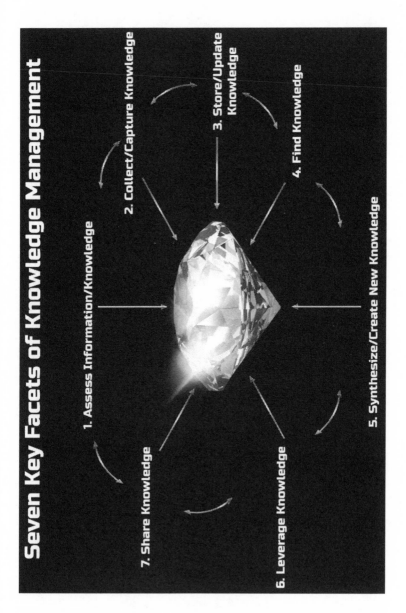

Seven Key Facets of KM

would be the first step. The subsequent steps would be storing this new knowledge, leveraging this knowledge into a new product, and sharing it with others.

FACET 1: ASSESS INFORMATION / KNOWLEDGE

One of the first activities when starting KM is to assess the current environment to understand the information and knowledge we have and what we don't have.

Some critical questions to ask include:

1. What information and knowledge do we have currently?

2. What information and knowledge are we missing?

3. How confident are we that we're talking with all of the right people when conducting our assessment?

Although it might appear that assessment could potentially end with this first facet, it is highly recommended that careful assessment of the current environment—as well as all of our assumptions and outcomes—take place continuously throughout the course of *all* KM initiatives.

FACET 2: COLLECT / CAPTURE KNOWLEDGE

This facet of KM involves collecting information and knowledge. In order to do anything significant with our knowledge, we must collect or capture it.

There can be overlap between Facet 1 and 2. We first assess our environment to determine what information and knowledge we want to collect. After the knowledge is captured, we should ensure that we have actually collected useful strategic knowledge before we store or update existing knowledge, which is the next facet.

Some questions to ask include:

1. Based on our initial assessment, is the information and knowledge we seek to collect appropriate, relevant and useful for our environment and goals? Is what we plan to collect *strategic* knowledge?

2. Is the source of our information and knowledge current, accurate and complete?

3. Do we completely understand the information and knowledge we're attempting to collect? Or do we need additional information or knowledge in order to perform the most optimal assessment?

4. Are we looking in all of the right places and asking the right people during this process?

5. In general, are we encouraging and making it easy for employees, partners and customers to provide feedback to us? Do we have a "Suggestion Box" to collect feedback and knowledge?

FACET 3: STORE / UPDATE KNOWLEDGE

Once the information and knowledge has been captured and confirmed that it is relevant for our environment and goals, we should either store it—or update existing knowledge.

It's critical to keep in mind when storing knowledge that it must be easily retrievable. If knowledge isn't easily discoverable when people search for it, there isn't much value in storing it. Therefore, the task of storage requires careful analysis and planning—and should compel us to ask questions such as:

1. *How* will the knowledge be stored? Will a text document, spreadsheet or database be used? If so, where will the file be saved? Will it be stored on a local hard drive, or on a network file share? Will a system such as SharePoint, Documentum, or other electronic repository be used?

2. Will the knowledge be stored in a database? If so, what fields will be used?

3. Will the knowledge be "tagged" with any keywords, key phrases, taxonomies or meta tags?

4. Are we ensuring that the knowledge will be easily discoverable when someone searches for it in the future?

FACET 4: FIND KNOWLEDGE

Once the knowledge has been collected, assessed and stored, it is important to be able to easily and effectively find it later.

The ability to easily search for and *find* knowledge is directly related to the manner in which it was stored. It is important to ensure that our searches are easy to perform and effectively produce the desired results.

Some questions to keep in mind when searching for and finding knowledge include:

1. Can we *easily find* exactly what we're searching for?

2. Are we able to specify what we're searching for in an intuitive manner—or is the process or system frustrating to use?

3. If our searches don't yield the expected results, are we using this new knowledge to redesign the process and methodology used to categorize, store and search for the knowledge?

You might have thought while reading about the first four key facets of KM that computers should be used to help collect, assess, store and find knowledge. Information technology *does* play an important role in Knowledge Management however, there is much more to KM than computers can currently handle by themselves. As knowledge workers, we still need to use our minds when managing information and knowledge. In addition, since KM is about *human* capital, we must constantly remember that people are always more important than technology. Let us keep this in mind as we look at the next three key facets of KM.

FACET 5: SYNTHESIZE / CREATE NEW KNOWLEDGE

The next facet involves synthesizing or integrating knowledge from various sources, which in turn creates fresh knowledge—sometimes, entirely new knowledge which has never been seen or shared before.

Some questions to undertake during this facet include:

1. Does our organization reward creativity and innovation?

2. Is our organization open to exploring and trying new ideas?

3. What are we doing with our new knowledge? Are we placing importance on it? Where is it being stored? Can others easily retrieve it?

4. Are we actually *synthesizing and integrating* knowledge in our organization—or are we just doing things as we've always done before?

FACET 6: LEVERAGE KNOWLEDGE

This facet involves the process of *actually utilizing* the knowledge we have gained. While this step might seem obvious, if we go out of our way to collect, assess, store, search and synthesize/create new knowledge, we should ensure that we are indeed using this knowledge in the most effective manner for our organization.

Some questions to ask to ensure that we're leveraging this knowledge to our greatest benefit include:

1. If our organization performs exit interviews, what is done with this knowledge once it has been collected? Do we attempt to address any negative situations? Are individuals or managers coached so that they can improve based on the information provided during exit interviews? Do we make a sincere effort to turn potentially negative feedback or situations into positive ones? At what level of the organization and with which stakeholders are these types of critical decisions made?

2. If we have a corporate program to train and educate people to improve their knowledge and skills, do we let people know about it? Are there regular enterprise-wide communications about these resources? Do our executives make an effort to integrate the knowledge and

skills that team members gained into their day-to-day job activities?

3. If we have created a knowledge repository, are people actually using the knowledge that we have carefully stored and made available to them? Do we keep metrics on how often people find and put the knowledge to use? Do we communicate regularly about these resources?

FACET 7: SHARE KNOWLEDGE

This final facet involves sharing knowledge in a variety of ways: via knowledge repositories (such as Knowledge Bases), documents, meetings, discussions, etc. Knowledge sharing is a fundamental facet of all KM efforts.

Some questions to ask when sharing knowledge include:

1. Are we sharing knowledge with the members of our immediate team?

2. Are we sharing knowledge with our peers?

3. Are we sharing knowledge with a larger group outside of our immediate organization?

This chapter covered one way to understand and apply Knowledge Management through the **Seven Key Facets of KM,** which also allows us to view KM in an IT-centric manner. These facets can be followed sequentially or in a non-sequential manner as well. In the next chapter, we will learn how to implement various tactics and techniques of KM through the **Seven Key Practice Areas of KM**. As you read about the practice areas, you will notice how these KM practices map back to each of the **Seven Key Facets of KM.**

3.

SEVEN KEY PRACTICE AREAS OF KM

This chapter will cover the various tools and techniques within the **Seven Key Practice Areas of KM**—some of which I've already referred to earlier.

A large number of tactical practices and techniques are utilized during the course of employing Knowledge Management. Although these seven areas highlight some of the most popular and effective practices, this list is ever-growing. Focusing on implementing KM initiatives found within the **Seven Key Practice Areas** will put you well on your way to implementing highly effective KM. These include:

1. On-Boarding and Off-Boarding
2. Facilitate Continuous Learning

3. Identify, Implement and Share Best Practices

4. Knowledge Repositories

5. Increase Innovation

6. Share and Collaborate

7. Measurement / Analysis

As the diagram on the next page illustrates, there is some degree of natural overlap between these practice areas. The larger and more complex a KM initiative is, the more likely that it will utilize techniques from multiple practice areas.

It's also important to note that—similar to the **Seven Key Facets of KM**—the techniques and tactics in each of the seven key practice areas can be applied in any order. The order is based on your KM goals, objectives and priorities.

PRACTICE AREA 1: ON-BOARDING AND OFF-BOARDING

We've already touched on the importance of providing an optimal on-boarding experience for all new people who join your organization. The most effective of these programs include elements such

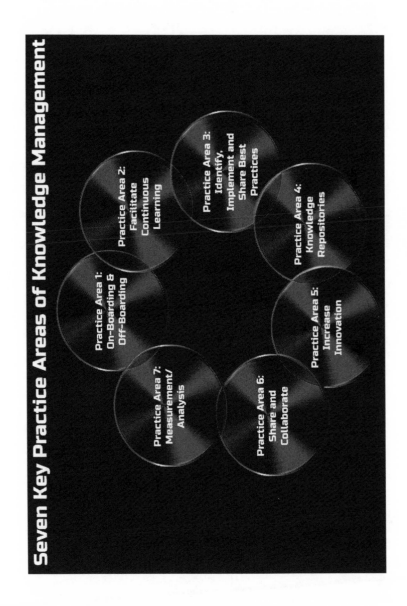

Seven Key Practice Areas of KM

as an official welcome to the company (i.e., a letter, conversation, mention in a company newsletter, or announcement at a company meeting), along with an Operations Manual, Play Book, Resource Guide, Welcome Packet, etc.—in short, any and all documents that record and share common processes, procedures, guidelines, names of important people and related organizations, definitions of acronyms, etc. (the development of which is a non-trivial task for a large organization!). These resources help transfer critical knowledge and quickly get new team members up to speed. They are also helpful for anyone who joins the team from another department or division.

It is also beneficial to create a "Buddy Program" that pairs new team members with existing, more experienced team members. This brings newcomers into the culture of the organization, provides a way for them to ask and get answers to questions, and helps people feel more welcomed and less overwhelmed. Pairing every team member with a buddy during the course of their tenure creates an atmosphere of friendship and supportive sharing. A well-run Buddy Program allows for a certain amount of flexibility, with each buddy deciding how often and how much time they spend with one another, although I recommend touching base at least on a weekly basis in the beginning.

Although plenty of learning will take place as buddies share knowledge and experiences, a Buddy Program is different than a Mentorship Program. The latter tends to be more difficult to set up and administer. Mentors typically take on the role of "teacher," where buddies tend to treat each other more as equals. In addition, many people feel that true mentorships can only happen in an organic fashion because of the personal chemistry that is often necessary in order for them to succeed.

In addition to on-boarding team members, organizations must also consider the other end of the spectrum—that is, what happens when a team member is about to leave the organization.

If a company is laying off employees, it is critical to explore all possibilities inside the organization—to place them in other parts of the company where possible and appropriate.

To retain the maximum amount of institutional knowledge during layoffs, it is also important that the decisions about who will be laid off include seeking feedback from multiple sources—to avoid a manager laying off the "wrong" employees.

To help ensure that knowledge doesn't "walk out the door" with employees who are leaving, it is wise to facilitate continuous learning and improvement through knowledge captured during an exit interview process. Companies can then use this rich source of information and knowledge to make organizational improvements. In a culture of continuous learning where the Lessons Learned process is conducted before, during and after major projects and events, the exit interview gives team members a chance to provide their final input regarding Lessons Learned.

When someone chooses to leave an organization, it makes sense for their manager to ask questions regarding the team member's key aspects of their job responsibilities, primary internal and external contacts, location of documented processes and procedures, names of people who may have received cross training, etc. These types of questions are separate from questions asked during an exit interview.

There are a variety of questions one can ask during exit interviews. However, some of the most valuable feedback from people leaving the organization is that which they've withheld until that point because it's too sensitive, difficult or awkward to share. For example, if a team member has a manager who is a workplace bully, who micromanages, or who takes credit for the work that others do, it may be difficult for the team member to share this information while still working under this person. However, people are more open to sharing sensitive or difficult feedback when they are leaving a company. People can be surprisingly candid because they know they have nothing to lose by sharing what they know—and might even be helping others still employed there, or people who might join in the future.

The exit interview should be performed in person if possible, and the questions should be designed to encourage sharing of any and all information and knowledge that can ultimately be used to improve the organization. After setting up an environment where the team member feels safe, here are a few examples of questions to ask:

1. Why are you leaving?

2. When and why did you start looking for a new job?

3. If you could change three things about the job or the company, what would you change?

4. What did you especially like about your job or the company?

5. What did you especially dislike about your job or the company?

6. Would you recommend this company to your friends as a great place to work? If not, why not?

7. Were you comfortable talking with your manager about issues and challenges in the workplace?

8. If you experienced issues, did you share your concerns with anyone prior to deciding to leave? How did they respond?

9. Is there anything your immediate manager could do to improve their skills and style?

10. Is there anything else that we should know about that could help us improve the company?

Start and finish the exit interview meeting on a positive note, thanking the person for their service and feedback and let them know that attempts will be made to address their concerns. Wish them well in their new endeavors.

Not only should this be an opportunity for team members to share their experience of the company prior to their departure; you want to create and execute a well-designed policy that spells out in detail what happens with the exit interview knowledge, by when and with whom, including any logic and reasoning utilized in the decision-making process. This important critical institutional knowledge must not only be captured, but wisely leveraged (the knowledge captured should not just be put in a file, ignored or discarded).

One Fortune 500 company specializing in medical devices, pharmaceuticals and consumer packaged goods increased employee retention by 20% simply by conducting exit interviews[6], and leveraging the knowledge once it was gathered. Companies that conduct exit interviews are seen as being mature and caring enough to expose themselves to criticism. When employees know that the company cares enough to ask why people are leaving—and that they actually choose to act upon such feedback—it creates an atmosphere of greater openness, satisfaction and productivity.

The following chart includes estimates of cost savings that can be achieved by implementing exit interviews—assuming a 10% annual turnover rate, an average annual salary of $100K, and that the cost of onboarding a new employee is 25% of their annual salary:

EXIT INTERVIEW COST SAVINGS	
# of Employees	Potential Annual Savings
5,000	$2.5 million
50,000	$25 million
100,000	$50 million
300,000	$150 million
3 million	$1.5 billion

---

6   Acuity Institute

PRACTICE AREA 2: FACILITATE CONTINUOUS LEARNING

A learning organization is one whose people continually expand the capacity to grow and create the results they truly desire. It's a place that nurtures new and expansive patterns of thinking, where collective aspiration is set free, and where people are continually *learning how to learn* together.[7]

A key element of a learning organization is that it is continually evolving—both as a whole, and as individual team members. Corporate learning programs play a major role in developing both groups' and individual team members' skills and knowledge.

Even without an official enterprise-wide learning program, employees can share and transition tacit to explicit knowledge through informal "Brown Bag" programs. In such scenarios, knowledge is shared on a variety of different topics, typically during lunch hour, either in a single physical location or online via an audio or video conferencing system. In addition to gaining information, participants are able to network with other employees while learning important

---

7   *The Fifth Discipline*, by Peter M. Senge

knowledge. Topics can range from learning about technologies, to projects, the work of other organizations inside the company—the sky is the limit. Any topic that would benefit from people sharing their knowledge is a potential topic for a Brown Bag program.

Another popular technique for sharing knowledge and facilitating continuous learning is called a knowledge café, which is a type of meeting which provides an open and creative conversation to surface collective knowledge, share ideas and insights and gain a deeper understanding of the topics and issues being discussed. The knowledge café method has multiple origins with links to other related methods such as The World Café. Elizabeth Lank developed the concept creating a physical and mobile café area in the 1990s. It has been popularized by Charles Savage and Entovation International, and in recent years by David Gurteen. Eunika Mercier-Laurent uses a similar principle for her Innovation cafés.[8]

One essential practice that helps individuals and groups learn how to work better together is awareness, team and communication-building tools, programs

8   Wikipedia, "Knowledge Café"

and workshops. Here are a few examples, some of which overlap the following three categories:

1. PERSONALITY ASSESSMENTS:

    1. StrengthsFinder[9] is a personal assessment that outlines an indivual's strengths. It promotes focusing on building strengths as opposed to improving weaknesses.

       StrengthsFinder is an great example of new knowledge in the Knowledge Age. For many years, the traditional approach to improving performance on the job is to help team members improve their areas of weakness. StrengthsFinder turns this approach on its head for a few reasons.

       First, a strength is defined as something you do that makes you feel strong, empowered and successful; a strength in this model is not necessarily something you are good at. Similarly, a weakness is not necessarily something you don't do well at but rather, a weakness is something you do that makes

---

9   Refer to strengthsfinder.com

you feel weak, disempowered and drained. The idea is that if we let our team members do more of what makes them feel strong and empowered, they will become even better in those areas and their level of job satisfaction will increase. And if we help team members do less of what makes them feel drained and disempowered, that will free them to focus on their strengths and what makes them feel empowered. It is a brilliant approach that can be utilized professionally as well as personally.

2. Myers-Briggs Type Indicator (MBTI)[10] is an introspective questionnaire designed to indicate psychological preferences in how people make decisions and perceive the world.

3. Hogan Assessments[11] is a series of assessments that are designed to help companies hire and develop people and teams.

4. DISC[12] is a commonly used tool to get to know oneself, others and behavior in interpersonal

---

10 Refer to myersbriggs.org

11 Refer to hoganassessments.com

12 Refer to wikipedia.org

situations better, which is designed to improve work productivity, teamwork and communication. The four letters in DISC stand for the four main behavioral traits of Dominance, Influence, Steadiness and Compliance.

5. The Enneagram in Business[13] is a company that focuses on utilizing the Enneagram—a model of human personality that is understood as a typology of nine interconnected personality types—to facilitate teambuilding, conflict resolution and decision making

2. COMMUNICATION SKILLS:

1. Crucial Conversations[14] is a book and training that helps facilitate improved conversations, especially when the stakes are high, opinions vary and emotions run strong.

2. Appreciative Inquiry[15] attempts to ask strengths-based questions and help people envision the future by leveraging what they already do well in order to foster positive

---

13 Refer to theenneagraminbusiness.com
14 Refer to vitalsmarts.com/crucialconversations
15 Refer to centerforappreciativeinquiry.net

relationships and improve the potential of a given person, organization or situation.

3. Nonviolent Communication (NVC)[16] is a communication process that focuses on three aspects of communication: self-empathy, other-empathy and honest self-expression.

4. Positive deviance[17] is a strengths-based approach to behavioral and social change based on the fact that in any environment, there are people whose uncommon but successful behaviors or strategies enable them to find better solutions to a problem than their peers, despite facing similar challenges and having no extra resources or knowledge than their peers.[18]

3. TEAM-BUILDING:

1. Formal and informal breakfasts, lunches and dinners can help people get to know one another and to build teamwork.

2. Various activities that take place as part of corporate meetings can be used to help

---

16 Refer to cnvc.org
17 Refer to positivedeviance.org
18 Wikipedia, "Positive deviance"

build teamwork. Two such examples are "icebreakers" and activities where team members share something about themselves that others might not know.

3. Volunteer opportunities in the community provide a venue for people to get to know one another in a volunteer setting, which helps facilitate the team-building process.

4. Outward Bound[19] is a global nonprofit organization whose programs foster personal growth, social skills and teamwork through challenging expeditions in the outdoors.

Since knowledge is understanding gained through experience, there are a few basic questions to regularly ask ourselves:

1. What are we understanding now that we didn't understand previously?

2. What experiences are we having?

3. What lessons are we learning?

---

19 Refer to outwardbound.org

As touched upon earlier, a critically important part of facilitating continuous learning is through leveraging of the Lessons Learned process. This process is sometimes called a post mortem, an after action review, an introspective, or a retrospective. But whatever label it's given, the underlying concept is to continuously learn *before, during and after* completion of a project, program, initiative or important event. This is an essential but sometimes overlooked process of converting tacit knowledge inside people's heads into valuable explicit knowledge that will better serve the organization.

This knowledge includes uncovering what the team did particularly well that we would want to continue in the future, what obstacles were faced, and what we didn't do well that we would want to do better in the future—all in the spirit of continuous improvement. Based on this knowledge, we can improve or create processes, increase efficiency in our work, coach people—in sum, make our work lives more productive and satisfying.

It is crucial to conduct the knowledge capture portion of the Lessons Learned process in a manner that makes it a positive experience for everyone involved. To set the tone of the meeting, it is helpful to send out "ground rules" to participants in advance. This allows attendees to start thinking before the meeting about how they want to state their feedback in a way that makes it actually useful. If possible, start and end with what went well. Here is a list of ground rules to follow:

LESSONS LEARNED MEETING GROUND RULES

1. The purpose of this gathering is to learn what worked well and what can be improved upon so that future projects can leverage our experience. Since knowledge is understanding gained from experience, the lessons learned process increases individual and institutional knowledge.

2. This process is an open and honest exchange of information for the benefit of the company.

3. This meeting is *not* about assigning blame and pointing fingers.

4. Ensure that all input to this process is constructive, positive and useful.

5. This focus should be on *behaviors and issues*, not on individuals.

One of the most important aspects of the Lessons Learned process makes use of something we first learned about in Chapter 2, Facet 4: Find Knowledge: to ensure that the knowledge captured is *searchable* in an easy to use, efficient, intuitive and highly effective manner.

Lessons should also be categorized and prioritized. As mentioned already, it is unwise to spend time and energy collecting valuable knowledge if you cannot easily leverage it later. Keeping this knowledge in an attainable place ensures that your organization will enjoy the benefits of lessons learned far beyond the project and the boundaries of the group involved.

Additionally, the more often we can capture and store Lessons Learned knowledge in a Lessons Learned Management System (LLMS), guided by a Lessons Learned Management Process (LLMP), the more often we can benefit from this knowledge. This process should be conducted regularly before, during and after events, projects, programs or initiatives are completed.

The British Petroleum (BP) company enhanced the traditional After Action Review concept to ensure that lessons were learned *before, during and after* as opposed to *only after* an event, project, program, initiative or crisis had taken place. As a result, BP documented a cost savings of $85 million[20] while conducting maintenance of their oil rigs. They discovered that by performing Lessons Learned before, during and after maintenance—as opposed to only after the maintenance was completed—they were able to share greater knowledge of issues, solutions and best practices across their oil rig locations, saving time and money.

PRACTICE AREA 3: IDENTIFY, IMPLEMENT AND SHARE BEST PRACTICES

A "best practice" is a method or technique that, through experience and research, reliably produces results considered to be superior to other methods and is therefore often used as a benchmark. Best practices and checklists are common ways of performing actions that can be used in multiple organizations. The identification and sharing of best practices is a powerful tool that every major KM program should strive to utilize to receive the maximum possible benefit of improved knowledge.

---

20 International Knowledge Management Institute

One example of a company that shared knowledge across their manufacturing facilities with great success is Ford Motor Company. They reduced assembly costs by $1.5 billion within a ten year period by encouraging cross-factory reviews and collaboration to build trust.[21]

Another example of the value of KM brought about through the sharing of best practices is Texas Instruments increasing efficiency across its 13 semiconductor wafer fabrication plants. They closed the gaps in the yield and productivity levels across multiple plants by sharing best practices via a best practice knowledgebase. They also created an incentive for the plants to work together by tying their bonuses to total capacity and productivity goals. This eliminated the need to build a new plant, generated $1.5 billion in annual increased fabrication capacity (in effect, a "new plant"), and saved the company $500 million in direct investment costs.[22]

The sharing of commonly accepted best practices is so powerful that it might be easy to overlook.

---

21 International Knowledge Management Institute
22 *If We Only Knew What We Know*, by O'Dell and Grayson

A year-long study related to this topic was led by the Harvard School of Public Health in collaboration with the World Health Organization (WHO) and a collection of hospitals in eight cities around the world. It was published by the New England Journal of Medicine in 2009[23]. The study demonstrated that the use of a simple surgical checklist during major operations can lower the incidence of deaths and complications by more than one third. The checklist is a single page that requires only a few minutes to complete and is intended to ensure safe delivery of anesthesia, appropriate preventive measures against infection, effective teamwork and other essential practices in operative care. The study estimated that if the WHO Surgical Safety Checklist was implemented in all operating rooms across the U.S., the annual cost-savings from the prevention of major complications would be $15 billion to $25 billion per year.[24] However, the checklist is such a simple concept that it was initially overlooked. Can you think of anything at your company that might be so simple and seemingly obvious that the team is actually overlooking it?

23 New England Journal of Medicine: *A Surgical Safety Checklist to Reduce Morbidity and Mortality in a Global Population,* January 29, 2009
24 Harvard School of Public Health: *Hospital pilot sites demonstrate surgical safety checklist drops deaths and complications by more than one third,* January 14, 2009

PRACTICE AREA 4:
KNOWLEDGE REPOSITORIES

It's essential to develop a knowledge repository or Knowledge Base that employees can easily and effectively search for processes and procedures, best practices, lessons learned and other useful information. Software development companies are actively trying to help facilitate this process through information technology solutions. One promising approach is to create a system where multiple repositories and databases can be searched and results displayed on one screen. Less advanced and comprehensive approaches include creating a smaller data repository with a smaller scope. Each approach—and many in between—can be extremely useful, with even more powerful solutions on the horizon. These repositories can be used by employees, call center agents, vendors, customers and others seeking answers to their questions.

Creating and constantly updating this database is what many people assume the extent of KM to be. Hopefully by now you understand that although creating repositories are of critical importance, they are only one component of KM. It can take a great deal of resources to accomplish properly. Due to these factors, until technology improves, I do not recommend attempting to create a comprehensive enterprise knowledge repository in a large organization as your first KM undertaking.

Another common and helpful practice that falls into this practice area is to create a Subject Matter Expert (SME) directory, expert directory or knowledge "yellow pages" that contain names and contact information of people within the company organized by subject matter, knowledge and/or skills. This type of resource is extremely valuable and can save an inordinate amount of time across your enterprise. The larger the organization, the larger the potential benefit. Examples include a software development company that creates a knowledge yellow pages for various types of programming skills or a company with offices around the world might create an SME directory that includes language speaking abilities, familiarity with customs and traditions in specific countries, etc.

According to a report by McKinsey & Company, workers spend 20% of their time searching for internal information or tracking down colleagues who can help them with specific tasks.[25] If we reduce time spent searching from 20% to 10%, a company with 100,000 employees could save more than $1 billion each year. Similarly, an organization with 3 million people could save more than $31 billion per year. Knowledge Management provides methods to make the process of searching for knowledge more efficient, productive and effective, and can save companies large amounts of time and money.

Here are a few other estimates of cost savings that can be achieved by decreasing time spent searching from 20% to 10%—assuming an annual number of work hours is 2,087 and the average rate is $50/hour:

COST SAVINGS DUE TO DECREASED TIME SPENT SEARCHING	
# of Employees	Potential Annual Savings
5,000	$52.17 million
50,000	$521.75 million
100,000	$1.04 billion
300,000	$3.13 billion
3 million	$31.31 billion

---

25 McKinsey & Company (2012)

PRACTICE AREA 5: INCREASE INNOVATION

Continuously striving to do things in a better way is a hallmark of good KM. Although there are certainly times when innovation "just happens," specific actions can be taken to help create an environment where people and teams feel supported, encouraged and rewarded for bringing forth fresh ideas.

One of the first and most critical steps in increasing innovation is to create an environment that promotes and rewards creative and innovative thinking. Team members need to know they are supported and encouraged to think innovatively in every aspect of their work. They need to know that it's OK to take risks and to fail without fear of being punished. This type of support must come from the highest level of the organization, and must be communicated frequently and consistently.

In addition to receiving support and encouragement for their creative and innovative ideas, team members should be rewarded as well. Rewards can come in the form of financial incentives as well as public recognition. Companies that do not yet have an official enterprise-wide Innovation Award Program should consider creating one. Such programs are important because they acknowledge and reward people for their creative and innovative ideas.

Fortunately, creating an Innovation Award Program is relatively straightforward. A first step is to secure support, commitment and funding for the program from the highest level of executive management. This includes determining who will administer the program, how many awards will be given, how often awards will be granted, the selection criteria, the dollar amount of each award and whether the winners will be recognized via email, newsletters, websites, during company meetings, etc. Then, a selection committee should be formed. This is the body of people that will review nominations and decide on the award winners. Once the program is launched (hopefully with great fanfare!), communications about the program should take place regularly and frequently so that team members know it's not just a passing interest.

Team members can nominate their peers for recognition of their creative and innovative ideas utilizing a standard nomination form. After the winners are chosen by the Innovation Award Program Selection Committee, they should be announced and publicized. The dollar amounts of the awards are not as important as the fact that there is a program in place where people are being encouraged, recognized and rewarded for their creative and innovative ideas.

If support from executive management is not immediately forthcoming, you can always create an Innovation Award Program at a lower level in the organization, which can be treated as a pilot. Once the pilot program is up and running, it may be easier to secure support from a higher level once management can see the value and know that the program will be properly executed.

The Lessons Learned process can also play an important role in helping create an environment that is open to diverse viewpoints and ideas. These new ideas and improvements made through learning of lessons can be a great source of creativity and innovation for any organization, because the existence of this process shows that the organization is open to and accepting of both hearing and using new ideas.

PRACTICE AREA 6:
SHARE AND COLLABORATE

Sharing information and knowledge is a linchpin activity of KM—and one that includes collaborating with other people and teams. This allows people to share information, knowledge and experiences and in the process, spread and maximize that knowledge to the greatest extent possible.

A powerful way to help transition tacit into explicit knowledge, collaborate and share at the same time is through knowledge networks such as KM Champions Teams, Communities of Practice, Communities of Interest and Communities of Action—all of which can take place within the company, in person or online.

A Community of Practice (CoP) is a group of people who share a craft or profession and who deepen their knowledge and experience by interacting on an ongoing basis. Members of a Community of Practice are active practitioners. Examples include Knowledge Management Communities of Practice, Project Management groups, a group of engineers looking to solve similar problems, doctors who work in a certain specialty area, etc.

A Community of Interest (CoI) is a group of people who share a common interest or passion, although are not necessarily experts or practitioners. Examples include photography, fishing, games, sports, etc.

A Community of Action (CoA) is a group of people who share the goal of using collective power to effect change in the world. Examples include issues like social justice, climate change, and poverty reduction.

There are many other types of communities such as Communities of Purpose, Circumstance, Place, Position, etc. Throughout this book, any reference to a "KM Community" includes KM Communities of Practice, KM Communities of Interest and KM Communities of Action and others, in the spirit of being inclusive and to deliberately bring these different communities or knowledge networks together.

In addition, we can also create a more informal "Knowledge Champions Team" or "KM Champions Team" to build teamwork and momentum as a precursor to a fully developed KM Community. For example, if you are just introducing KM to your company and you have a few people who are interested in how Knowledge Management can be utilized, it might not make sense to launch a KM Community. Creating this kind of group is only the beginning; in order for it to be successful in the long run, you must carefully tend to the community. For instance, people who ask questions in your online KM Community should receive a helpful and timely response. However, all it takes to create a Knowledge Champions Team is a few people who are interested in the subject and agree to meet and take action to move KM forward in their organization.

The Royal Dutch Shell Group attributes more than $200 million in cost savings in 2002 by implementing online communities with thousands of members worldwide to share knowledge and best practices internally.[26]

Another oil company, Chevron, credits sharing and managing knowledge with a reduction of operating costs in the amount of $2 billion per year.[27] This includes sharing of best practices for managing energy use, managing capital efficiency, improv-

---

26 International Knowledge Management Institute
27 Kenneth T. Derr, Chairman of the Board and Chief Executive Officer, Chevron Corporation

ing high-cost functions ranging from catalytic cracking to plant maintenance, improvement of safety performance, increasing oil and gas well drilling performance, and exchanging ideas on valuing and promoting diversity.

An additional highly effective practice to facilitate collaboration and sharing is to use knowledge networks enabled with social software. These collaborative sharing tools include chat, instant messaging, audio conferencing, video conferencing, wikis, forums, blogs, social bookmarking services and social networks. These powerful technologies are especially useful in situations where team members are geographically dispersed or when they work from home.

PRACTICE AREA 7:
MEASUREMENT / ANALYSIS

One of the most common maxims in business is that "you can't manage what you can't measure." It is not enough to expect results; we must *inspect what we expect*. While it is not necessarily easy or even possible to measure everything that has value, measuring our KM activities through objective metrics is very important, valuable—and completely doable.

Analysis and reporting of metrics and knowledge overall is naturally of critical importance.

Our most important KM metrics will focus on the direct end results of KM: operational efficiency, cost reduction, risk reduction, and competitive advantage achieved through innovations. ROI metrics are of vital importance.

In addition to measuring the end results of KM, we can also measure and analyze our business environment by performing knowledge audits to identify sources, uses and flows of knowledge. KM assessments can be used to gauge the quality and capabilities of Knowledge Management, including the quality and effectiveness of our KM initiatives. By asking yourself the questions posed throughout this book, you will organically begin to perform a cursory KM assessment of your environment and initiatives. Finally, we can use benchmarking to compare performances across different organizations or departments and learn from the results by adopting outstanding practices.

This chapter examined the **Seven Key Practice Areas of KM,** each of which contains multiple tactics and techniques for implementing KM in your organization. In the next chapter, you will learn how to understand, structure, implement and monitor your KM initiatives according to the **Seven Key Pillars of KM** while utilizing the **Seven Key Practice Areas of KM**.

"We are drowning in information but starved for knowledge."

—John Naisbitt
author of *Megatrends*

4.

SEVEN KEY PILLARS OF KM

Given the many different tactical methods and techniques of KM, it might feel as though we have the potential to drown in too much information. The knowledge contained in this chapter and throughout the rest of this book will simplify and help you understand how to implement KM in your organization.

In Chapter 2, you learned about the **Seven Key Facets of Knowledge Management**—which can be viewed as an IT-centric way of describing the mechanics of KM. Through the **Seven Key Practice Areas**, you learned about common tactical KM practices and techniques you can employ to gain the value of KM in your organization.

However, more than a list of tactical practices and techniques is needed. Otherwise, our KM efforts will be piecemeal, not integrated nor holistic. This is where the **Seven Key Pillars of KM** come into play—and provide the following:

1. A framework to systematically uncover organizational issues and opportunities that KM can help address.

2. A way to organize and prioritize KM initiatives.

3. A system for monitoring and measuring the status and effectiveness of KM initiatives.

The general idea is to use the **Seven Key Pillars of KM** to identify, create and implement various KM initiatives. Ideally, we would create one or more initiatives *within each* of the seven pillars—which are as follows:

1. Reduce Knowledge Discovery Time

2. Improve Knowledge Processes

3. Foster Knowledge-Based Teamwork

4. Integrate / Leverage New Knowledge

Seven Key Pillars of Knowledge Management

Increased Efficiency, Productivity and Effectiveness

Pillar 1	Pillar 2	Pillar 3	Pillar 4	Pillar 5	Pillar 6	Pillar 7
Reduce Knowledge Discovery Time	Improve Knowledge Processes	Foster Knowledge-Based Teamwork	Integrate /Leverage New Knowledge	Collaborate /Share Knowledge	Manage Knowledge Risks	Promote 3-Way Enterprise Knowledge

Individual and Organizational Knowledge
Organizational Change Management

Seven Key Pillars of KM

5. Collaborate / Share Knowledge

6. Manage Knowledge Risks

7. Promote 3-Way Enterprise Knowledge

The diagram on the previous page is a graphical depiction of these pillars. You may notice there is some natural overlap between each of the pillars as you read and think about them. This emphasizes the notion introduced at the very beginning of the book—that KM contains overlapping and non-linear elements. The larger and more complex a KM initiative is, the greater the likelihood that it will span across multiple pillars. This is by design and can be particularly helpful when we're identifying issues and opportunities that KM can help address. We can use these key pillars at any organizational level or at the level of a single project.

FOUNDATION OF INDIVIDUAL AND ORGANIZATIONAL KNOWLEDGE, AND ORGANIZATIONAL CHANGE MANAGEMENT

We can see when looking at the diagram on the previous page that the *foundation* consists of individual and organizational/institutional knowledge. This is true for every organization. Not only do individuals possess knowledge; the organization or institution itself also has *collective* knowledge. An organization's knowledge is more than just the sum of its members' knowledge and goes back to the birth of the organization. Each of the seven key pillars is built on the foundation of these two types of knowledge.

We can also see from the diagram that the foundation includes organizational change management. You will learn more about the concept of change management in Chapter 6—but to summarize here, this deals with successfully shepherding change through the organization, including dealing with human dynamics and psychological issues associated with change. Without proper change management, KM initiatives are in danger of either never taking off, or faltering after being launched. Success comes from a strong foundation of organizational change management that is implemented across all seven key pillars of KM—each of which will be discussed in detail in the following pages.

PILLAR 1: REDUCE KNOWLEDGE DISCOVERY TIME

One of the fundamental tenets of Knowledge Management is to *reduce the time we spend discovering and rediscovering knowledge.* Our KM efforts should make it as easy as possible to deliver the right knowledge to the right person at the right time. Once a person or organization has discovered knowledge, we should be able to reduce—or even eliminate—the need to do so again. We want to minimize the time we spend discovering and rediscovering knowledge to the greatest extent possible. One essential step in doing this is to transfer all undocumented mission-critical tacit knowledge to explicit, documented knowledge.

One simple yet powerful way to reduce time spent discovering and rediscovering knowledge is to create a resource for new team members to learn processes and procedures for getting work done in their organization, including names of key people and their contact information. As mentioned before, new team members could be given an Operations Manual, a Welcome Packet or a Resource Guide, etc. or could be given access to a website where all of this knowledge would be stored and easily retrieved. When team members need to refresh their memory on a process they don't perform very often, they simply go back to the website, Operations Manual, Resource Guide or Welcome Packet, etc. Without tools like these, new team members might have to ask their co-workers or managers—all of which takes time.

In addition to improving efficiency, productivity and effectiveness, an added benefit to having this resource is ensuring that everyone performs the work in a consistent manner.

Some questions to ask when reducing knowledge discovery and rediscovery include:

1. Do we provide new team members with onboarding and knowledge transfer resources such as an Operations Manual, Resource Guide, Welcome Packet or website(s) so they can "hit the ground running"?

2. Do we have an internal corporate Knowledge Base (KB) where team members can find key knowledge about the company—such as organization charts, organizational charters, information about benefits, policies, procedures,

self-service customer support, answers to commonly asked questions, etc.? If so, is it updated regularly and by whom?

3. Do we perform a Lessons Learned process before, during and after major events or projects/initiatives are completed? Do we make it easy for others to search through this knowledge so they can benefit from what others have already learned?

PILLAR 2: IMPROVE KNOWLEDGE PROCESSES

This pillar focuses on identifying and executing opportunities for *improving existing knowledge processes*. Since processes to perform work tasks almost always involve some type of knowledge, this pillar includes the improvement of processes or procedures.

Some questions we can ask ourselves when executing on this pillar are:

1. Are we using any processes that we could improve?

2. What mechanisms are we using to seek out and reward suggestions for process improvements,

in the spirit of continuous improvement in our organization?

PILLAR 3: FOSTER KNOWLEDGE-BASED TEAMWORK

Teams of people that work well together will enjoy greater productivity, effectiveness and team spirit. This pillar includes implementing KM initiatives that foster teamwork by leveraging knowledge of and from one another.

Some questions to ask during this process are:

1. As first mentioned in Chapter 3 (Practice Area 1: On-Boarding and Off-Boarding), do we have an official or unofficial "Buddy Program" where new team members are encouraged to interact and be "buddies" with an existing team member? Buddy Programs help create ways for increasing knowledge transfer and that strengthens relationships.

2. Do we have regular team-building programs, offsite outings, etc.? Monthly or quarterly programs that increase knowledge of other team members and build teamwork are an important

way to increase team member satisfaction and productivity.

3. Do we have any programs that encourage sharing of knowledge about each other? For example, some organizations have a "featured employee" section on their website or in their newsletters, etc.

4. Do we have programs that encourage understanding ourselves and others? Such programs increase our sensitivity and understanding of ourselves and others, minimize friction between people and teams, and help our teams and organizations be more effective. Chapter 3: Seven Key Practice Areas of KM includes some examples of these (such as Myers-Briggs, DISC and StrengthsFinder among others).

5. Do we have an organization-wide Innovation Award Program that encourages and rewards innovation and creativity?

6. Do we have a Knowledge Champions Team or a KM Community (as described in Chapter 3, Practice Area 6)?

PILLAR 4: INTEGRATE / LEVERAGE NEW KNOWLEDGE

This pillar encourages *knowledge integration*, which takes place when we synthesize knowledge from different sources or perspectives. It also includes integrating and leveraging this new knowledge into our work environments. Innovation and creativity play important roles in integrating and effectively utilizing knowledge in our work environments.

Some questions to ask when integrating/leveraging new knowledge include:

1. Do we have programs or initiatives that encourage continual learning (such as corporate professional development and training programs), especially when paired with encouragement and support to utilize this newly gained knowledge?

2. Do we have an organization-wide Innovation Award Program that encourages and rewards innovation and creativity—even if it means there may be occasional failures?

PILLAR 5: COLLABORATE / SHARE KNOWLEDGE

You've learned the importance of sharing knowledge as one of the fundamental tenets of the art and science of Knowledge Management. When one person or organization gains valuable knowledge, it becomes even more beneficial when they share it with others.

One step beyond sharing knowledge to benefit others is *collaborating with* others. We not only share knowledge by deliberately making an effort to pool resources and ideas with other people and organizations; we can continually learn from one another and fine tune and evolve the knowledge as well as our relationships.

It is, of course, important to give credit where it is due in an environment where people are constantly sharing and collaborating. Failing to acknowledge the appropriate sources of knowledge and information can pose unnecessary roadblocks to successful KM and cause people to hesitate to share their knowledge. So if some of your KM activities are inspired by someone else, *say so!* Everyone will feel respected and it will encourage further sharing and collaborating.

Some questions to ask when collaborating/sharing knowledge include:

1. Are we actively and deliberately sharing our knowledge with other people and teams, inside and outside of our own company?

2. Do we have an active and intentional program that encourages collaboration with other people and organizations?

3. If we are actively sharing knowledge with others, what methods do we use? Can we increase sharing through other means?

4. Do we encourage the use of best practices?

5. Do we have a "Brown Bag" program where we give employees a chance to share knowledge casually over lunch—either in person and/or online?

PILLAR 6: MANAGE KNOWLEDGE RISKS

This pillar requires us to identify knowledge-related risks and implement KM initiatives to mitigate them. Examples of knowledge risks include lack of key

knowledge within and outside of our work environments that could lead to loss of business opportunities, knowledge that isn't being shared among
co-workers, lack of an exit interview process which
prevents valuable information from leaving the company (through retirements, people leaving the company for other opportunities, etc.) and anything that
can potentially impede providing the right knowledge
to the right person at the right time. Undocumented
mission-critical tacit knowledge should be transitioned to documented explicit critical knowledge,
otherwise it is a knowledge risk.

Some questions to ask when managing knowledge
risks include:

1. Do we have a significant number of people
   who will soon retire? If so, what is our plan to
   ensure that we don't lose these team members'
   valuable knowledge when they leave?

2. Do we have a significant number of people
   in one part of our organization that will soon
   be downsized? If so, what is our plan to
   ensure that we don't lose these team members'

valuable knowledge? Do we have a plan to help these people find other positions within our company? Have we created a succession plan?

3. Do we have knowledge gaps in our environment? For example, if our organization creates proposals to generate new business, do we have all of the knowledge we need to create the best possible proposal?

4. In general, does our organization share knowledge—or do we tend to "protect" it to the point of keeping it to ourselves? If we're using KM at the project level, do we have team members that are not sharing their knowledge?

5. Do we have effective on-boarding and off-boarding programs, including capturing knowledge via exit interviews? When we fail to do this, valuable knowledge literally walks out the door—information that includes the perspective of their experiences, opinions of team members and management, suggestions for improvement, etc.

PILLAR 7: PROMOTE 3-WAY ENTERPRISE KNOWLEDGE

Promoting enterprise-wide knowledge works in three ways. First, if we have valuable knowledge at the highest level of our organization that we need to follow, it should be shared, promoted and utilized it in a top-down fashion. As the enterprise gains knowledge, so does each other part of the organization as knowledge is shared in a top-down fashion.

The second way to promote knowledge is to share what we learn in our own immediate organizations upward to the larger enterprise. The bottom-up sharing of knowledge upwards allows the organization as a whole to benefit from our knowledge.

The third way to promote knowledge is to share it laterally with our peers. This is particularly important if our organization doesn't have a process in place for sharing information upward. For example, if our organization does not have an effective Lessons Learned Management Process and system to support it as described in Chapter 3, then we don't have a proven or helpful way to feed knowledge upwards other than simply notifying our direct manager. In this case, it would be particularly important to share the knowledge laterally to our peers to ensure maximum benefit to the organization.

Some questions to ask when promoting enterprise knowledge include:

1. Is enterprise-wide knowledge shared effectively from the top of the organization down? Are processes, standards, regulations, and best practices easily accessible and widely known?

2. Do we encourage people and teams to spread innovative and useful ideas upwards and laterally in the organization to encourage sharing across the enterprise?

3. Do we regularly conduct Lessons Learned sessions before, during and after major events, projects or milestones, to collect and share this knowledge for the benefit of other people and teams? If so, are others aware of this resource? What do we do with the knowledge once it is captured? Can others easily search for and access it, so they too can benefit from this knowledge?

4. If our company is not yet harnessing the power of KM, are we asking management why not? Are we expressing our desire for the use of KM and optimizing human capital up the management chain? Are we actively suggesting improvements to management?

THE RESULTS: INCREASED EFFICIENCY, PRODUCTIVITY AND EFFECTIVENESS

When executed properly, implementing initiatives within each of the **Seven Key Pillars of KM** will result in greater efficiency, productivity and effectiveness—and as a result, lower cost. Our KM initiatives allow us to optimize our organization's human capital and intellectual assets. Increased efficiency, productivity and effectiveness, and lower costs are all examples of the fruits of our KM labor.

THREE WAYS TO USE THE SEVEN KEY PILLARS OF KM:

1. Systematically uncover organizational issues and opportunities that KM can help address by going through each of the seven pillars and asking some of the questions posed earlier. Thoughtfully thinking about these will likely

lead you to additional questions—all of which will help identify issues and opportunities that KM can help resolve. For example, one of the questions from Pillar 3 that we can ask is if we have a Buddy Program to help welcome new team members and facilitate teamwork and informal sharing of knowledge. As a result of going through the seven key pillars and asking this question, we might realize that we have identified an opportunity.

2. For each issue/opportunity you identified in the previous step, create an initiative or project that can help address the challenge, and assign it to one of the seven pillars. If you assign more than one KM initiative for a pillar, list them in priority from highest to lowest. To continue with the example from number one, we identified the issue/opportunity of creating a Buddy Program. As a result, we add creation of a Buddy Program as a KM initiative in Pillar 3: Foster Knowledge-Based Teamwork and Pillar 5: Collaborate/Share Knowledge.

3. To monitor and measure your KM initiatives' status and effectiveness, create a matrix that

shows each of the seven pillars. Within each pillar, list your KM initiatives in order from highest to lowest priority. Then, for each initiative, use a color-coded process to indicate the status (one common approach is to use red, green and yellow to reflect the overall status). You can also give each pillar an overall color-coded status. You can use this as a simple KM "dashboard" for your overall KM Program. Over time, these dashboards can be evolved to include more information such as an indicator to measure the amount of tacit knowledge being converted into explicit knowledge, initiatives as they map to each of the Seven Key Facets of KM, etc. For an example of a simple knowledge dashboard with KM initiatives, please refer to Chapter 10: Seven Step KM Strategy Example Walkthrough.

By systematically using the **Seven Key Pillars of KM**, and constantly facilitating change by implementing change management, you can identify issues and areas of opportunity. You can organize and prioritize your KM initiatives pillar by pillar and can view the status of your initiatives using a KM dashboard. It's simple, effective—and can even be fun!

Next we will learn how to utilize the **Seven Key Facets of KM**, the **Seven Key Practice Areas of KM** and the **Seven Key Pillars of KM** in a variety of different areas through the **Seven Key Lenses of KM**.

5.

SEVEN KEY LENSES OF KM

So far, the focus has been on how to utilize Knowledge Management in the world of business and commerce. As mentioned previously, one of the most extraordinarily valuable things about KM is that we can use it in many situations and environments. Similar to having a set of prescription eyeglasses for reading, another for long-distance viewing and yet another set for the outdoor sun, we can use different KM lenses depending on our situation.

Here are the **Seven Key Lenses of Knowledge Management**:

1. Business
2. Organizations and Institutions

3. Projects

4. Personal Lives

5. Local Communities

6. Global Community

7. Culture/Society

These seven lenses are depicted visually in the diagram on the following page.

LENS 1: BUSINESS

This, of course, is the lens we've been using in the book thus far—so you're likely already pretty familiar with it! Some questions to ask when using the Business lens include:

1. Are we satisfied with the overall level of success at our company, including how much profit we're making?

2. Are we satisfied with our overall level of productivity, efficiency, effectiveness and administrative costs?

3. Do we believe we are maximizing human capital to the fullest extent possible?

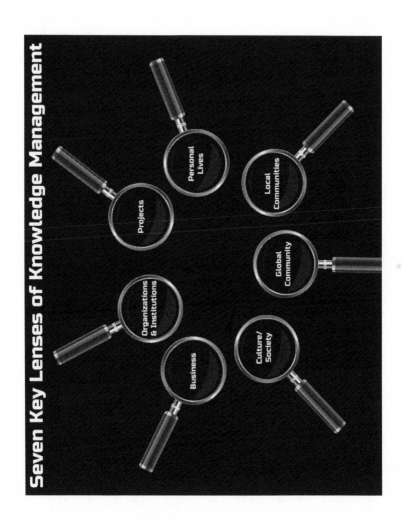

Seven Key Lenses of KM

4. Is our organization generally a source of positive energy? Are team members satisfied and proud to work here, and consider it a good company to work for?

5. Have we established a Knowledge Champions Team or KM Community? If so, has it been carefully tended to, with adequate communications, awareness, facilitation and support? If we already have a KM Community in our organization, is it easily accessible across the entire company? Are we connected and involved with related KM Communities outside our organization?

LENS 2: ORGANIZATIONS AND INSTITUTIONS

Every organization can benefit from ways to maximize its human capital and operate with greater efficiency, productivity, and effectiveness, at a lower cost. KM can be used in:

- Nonprofit organizations
- Educational institutions
- Religious institutions
- Civic and community service organizations

- Social organizations
- All areas of the government (including the military)
- Non-governmental organizations (NGOs)

Some questions to ask when using the Organizations and Institutions lens include:

1. Is our organization's mission being fulfilled in the most efficient and effective manner possible?

2. Is our human capital being maximized to the greatest extent possible?

3. In an environment of limited resources, are we utilizing our resources of people, materials, finances, time and energy wisely?

4. Is our organization producing the best possible outcomes?

5. Has a Knowledge Champions Team or KM Community been established? If so, has it been carefully tended to, with adequate communications, awareness, facilitation and support? If we already have a KM Community in our

organization, is it easily accessible across the entire institution? Are we involved with related KM Communities outside our organization?

You've probably noticed that we can use many of the same tools, techniques and questions we use when applying KM in a business environment, in any organization. However, we do so with a decreased focus on profit and an increased focus on the effectiveness and efficiency in fulfilling our mission.

Where a for-profit organization would use KM to focus narrowly on increasing financial resources (via the Business lens), a nonprofit or social profit organization could focus on assessing the effectiveness of its actions compared to its mission. We might also focus on other "bottom line" items such as ensuring employee, customer, and partner satisfaction, as well as the satisfaction level of the communities in which we serve and operate.

An example of a nonprofit organization that utilizes Knowledge Management is the American Red Cross. In order to identify and promote innovative and successful best practices, they implemented a system to share these best practices internally. After only one year in operation, the system grew from containing a few methods to a system that contained best practices from every line of service and every function. Their powerful best practices system increases efficiency, and reduces time and costs.

An example of another nonprofit organization that utilizes KM is Everyday Democracy, an organization that focuses on collecting and sharing the lessons learned of citizen engagement so that these best practices can spread. An example of a powerful lesson they learned and shared as a best practice is when starting public dialogue, it is vital to begin by getting to know each other to build trust. Without starting at the personal level, lack of trust can derail the dialogue.

Another lesson they learned and shared was that issues of racial equality are inextricably intertwined.

Therefore, racial equality must be addressed as a root cause during the course of discussing civic engagement and community change.[28]

28 Carrie Boron, former Organizational Effectiveness and Learning Officer for Everyday Democracy

One more example of a large-scale nonprofit organization that utilizes KM is the United Nations system.[29] Groups within the UN system that utilize various elements of KM include the Food and Agriculture Organization (FAO), the International Labour Organization (ILO), the International Maritime Organization (IMO), the World Food Programme (WFP) and the World Health Organization (WHO).

LENS 3: PROJECTS

Whether working with small, medium or large teams, anyone who manages projects can benefit from the discipline of Knowledge Management. KM is a powerful tool that project managers can employ to ensure that projects are executed on time, within budget and according to scope. Some questions to ask when using the Projects lens include:

1. Keeping the project's size and complexity in mind, ensuring easy access to our project documentation can be of critical importance. Do we have a knowledge repository for our project?

---

29 United Nations, "Knowledge Management in the United Nations System," by Juan Luis Larrabure, United Nations Joint Inspection unit

2. Do we conduct a Lessons Learned process before, during and after completing projects? Do we share this knowledge up and across the organization? Do we operate in the spirit of continuous improvement?

3. Are *knowledge transfers* happening—does everyone on the team have easy access to the knowledge they need to perform their jobs most efficiently? Are team members sharing knowledge freely?

4. It is common during long-term projects for the team to change over time, with people joining and leaving at various points. Do we have an effective project on-boarding process that allows new team members to move through the learning curve as quickly as possible? Do we have an exit interview process to capture and leverage knowledge when people leave the team or company?

5. During the course of delivering a project, it is common to observe the need for improved processes or procedures—either with work taking place within the team itself or with another team. Do we pursue documenting and

sharing them? If the improvements are out-side of our span of control, do we follow up with the appropriate people who can make the improvements—or is this valuable knowledge slipping through the cracks?

6. Do we encourage and reward project team members to think creatively and innovatively?

7. Do we run meetings efficiently and effectively (by inviting the appropriate people, starting and ending on time, treating and distribut-ing an agenda in advance of the meeting that includes topics, along with time limits for each topic, appointing someone to keep track of time and ensuring topics are covered, docu-menting and sending out meeting minutes afterwards that include topics discussed, deci-sions made, action items taken by whom and when they are due, etc.)?

8. Do we merely have a collection of people—or do we have a finely-tuned team with members that are truly collaborating with one another? How well do team members know each other? Do we engage in team-building activities?

9. Do we resolve issues with non-team players,

or do we let one person negatively impact the project?

10. Do we actively utilize KM in our projects? One easy way to incorporate KM into our efforts is to insert "KM Checkpoints" at the end of each phase, stage, or gate of the project. A KM Checkpoint can be as simple as performing a Lessons Learned process. Asking ourselves "What have we learned?" is valuable not just at the end of a project, but all throughout the course of a project.

11. Do we create an environment for people to identify, share and act on new knowledge?

12. We can expect during the course of a project that team members take time off for vacations, illness or to otherwise leave the company unexpectedly. We can plan in advance to minimize disruption to the project. Do we keep a record of planned time off? Do we have backup plans for when certain team members are not available?

13. Is there a Knowledge Champions Team or existing KM Community that can help team members learn and share knowledge?

LENS 4: PERSONAL LIVES

KM can be used to help us achieve a successful, prosperous and fulfilling career but it can also be used in our friendships and relationships, including love and romance. Although currently there is a relatively small amount of written material on the subject, the growing interest in Personal Knowledge Management (PKM) is very promising and exciting. The basic goal is to leverage all of the knowledge available to us in order to live happier, healthier and more productive lives.

My first book, *The Pieces of Our Puzzle: An Integrated Approach to Personal Success and Well-Being*,[30] provided a holistic synthesis of the world's major schools of psychology. Although the first edition was not written in the language of KM, it is very KM-like in that it aims to help people learn how to maximize personal success and well-being, one of the key goals of using the Personal Lives lens.

The key diagram from the book, shown on the following page, shows seven different components. Each component is a puzzle unto itself, and all of these together represent the puzzle of our own lives. Understanding each

---

30 Although the first edition is no longer in print, a second edition is underway. To be notified when the second edition is available, click here http://www.brenthunter.tv/#!the-pieces-of-our-puzzle/w1bok

of the individual components and all of them together leads to greater personal success and well-being.

Here is the diagram:

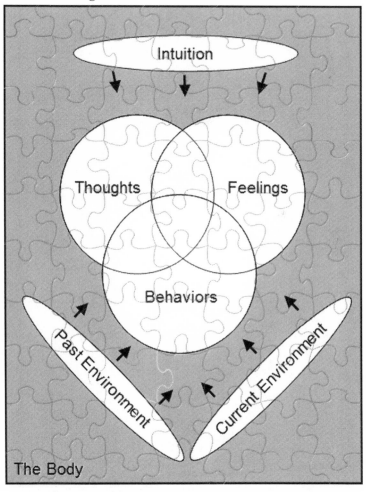

Main Diagram from *The Pieces of Our Puzzle* book

The Pieces of Our Puzzle summarized the following concepts:

1. Who we are today is shaped based on a complex combination of the following seven components, similar to the pieces of a puzzle:

    i. Past experiences

    ii. Current environment and experiences

    iii. Thoughts

    iv. Emotions

    v. Behaviors

    vi. The physical body

    vii. Sense of intuition

2. Based on what is happening in the present moment, it is important to look at each of the above pieces to understand how each one fits into our lives today. We can ask ourselves a series of questions and think about the experiences that have shed light onto each of these seven different pieces. As a result of increasing knowledge and awareness of the relative importance and significance of the various

pieces, we gain personal knowledge, self-mastery, productivity and greater inner peace.

Some questions to ask when using the Personal Lives lens include:

1. What is my personal life mission?

2. Am I learning with each relationship in my life? What exactly am I learning?

3. Am I learning with each interaction I have with another person?

4. What specific improvements am I making in my life?

5. Am I learning through experience, so that I'm not repeating the same behaviors or experiencing the same unwanted outcomes?

6. Does it feel good to know I'm working things out using sound logic and reasoning in my personal life?

7. What practices do I use to achieve peace of mind? Do I have a meditation practice? Do I exercise or practice any form of yoga?

8. Do I have any special talents? If so, what am I doing to cultivate and grow these abilities? What is my kryptonite—anything that can hinder me from exercising these abilities? What is my spinach—anything that can help support and accelerate my "superpowers," similar to the way spinach helped fuel Popeye's superhero abilities?

9. It makes sense when using the Personal Lives lens that we should leverage all available sources of knowledge to achieve maximum benefit. Learning about our own individual needs, desires and internal dynamics is of great importance to living a happy, successful life. We can gain knowledge through the experience of counseling and therapy and through self-help resources. Am I taking advantage of these professional services in my life? If so, am I fully utilizing all of the knowledge I've gained?

10. One of the most amazing tools we have to maximize the use and leverage of knowledge are computers and mobile devices. These allow us to easily access dictionaries and encyclopedias, store and retrieve names and contact

information, receive reminders, use notepads, use to-do lists, utilize mind maps, interact with social networks, and much more. Am I using technology to harness and maximize knowledge for the purpose of improving my life?

11. What am I doing to reduce my own learning curve in various areas of my life? In Chapter 6, you will learn more about change management, including why it is a critically important part of reducing the duration of learning curves. Once you see the Kübler-Ross Change Curve diagram on page 124, make an attempt to view the diagram from the perspective of your own personal life, as the dynamics are the same.

12. Similar to the way organizations gain knowledge and value by establishing, connecting and sharing with other KM Communities, we can gain value as individuals. Am I involved in any communities or social circles where I can share my knowledge, expertise and passion, and gain from the knowledge, expertise and passion of others? This includes social organizations as well as civic and community service

organizations such as the Boy Scouts, Girl Scouts, 4-H, Kiwanis International, Rotary International, Lions Clubs International, United Nations Association, and many more.

LENS 5: LOCAL COMMUNITIES

A local community can be defined as the immediate people beyond our family in our town, village or city. We can also expand that definition of local to include people at the regional, state and national levels.

Some questions to ask when using the Local Communities lens include:

1. Are we using all of the available knowledge at our disposal to improve the lives of people in our community?

2. Are we using KM to improve race relations and to bridge divides in our community?

3. Is there a local Knowledge Champions Team or KM Community? If so, has it been carefully tended to, with adequate communications, awareness, facilitation and support? At the local, regional, state and national level, a

THE POWER OF KM

network of KM Communities would be most useful as a method to collect, assess, store, find, synthesize, leverage and share knowledge collectively.

LENS 6: GLOBAL COMMUNITY

This lens focuses on issues and opportunities related to the smooth and harmonious system that currently supports our global community—the community of human beings living on the planet at this historic time. Since the world is a huge place, the application of KM at the level of the global community is also large and complex. But when guided by the holistic strategy described in this book, we can sort out all of our issues in a harmonious and effective manner through conversation, dialogue and diplomacy.

The world is expected to invest $90 trillion in infrastructure in cities, land use and energy between 2015 and 2030.[31] A brilliant example of the use of a powerful KM technique to help resolve global challenges is the creation of the Global Infrastructure Forum[32] —an initiative to create a global platform for knowledge

31 CNN: "The $90 trillion question" (October 19, 2015)
32 The Brookings Institution: "Driving sustainable development through better infrastructure: Key elements of a transformation program" (July, 2015)

exchange and action. It will identify and address infrastructure gaps, highlight opportunities for investment and cooperation, and work to ensure that projects are environmentally, socially and economically sustainable.[33] It is but one exciting example of harnessing the extraordinary value of KM in the Knowledge Age.

Some questions to ask when using the Global Community lens include:

1. Are our efforts to ensure that we are meeting people's basic needs of food, water and shelter effective and efficient?

2. Are we adequately acting as shepherds to protect the environment in which we live? At a minimum, are we not making the environment worse than it already is? Are our methods of producing and delivering food and water effective and efficient, and not damaging to the environment?

3. Since the vast majority of people around the world want to live in harmony, are all of our efforts toward this goal effective and efficient?

---

33 United Nations, "Countries reach historic agreement to generate financing for new sustainable development agenda"

4. If we believe knowledge is valuable, then it naturally makes sense that education is valuable. Are we making the necessary efforts to ensure that everyone receives an adequate education?

5. How are we helping people around the world live in a culture of law and order?

6. Is our system of international currency trading effective, efficient and serving the needs of all? If we were to use KM to improve the efficiency of the $5.3 trillion that is presently traded every day in foreign exchange markets worldwide[34] by just 1%, we could save an incredible $53 billion *every day*. If we multiply this amount by 365 days per year, this amounts to an impressive $20.44 trillion per year! Imagine what a $20.44 trillion annual budget could do to help improve the quality of life for billions of people worldwide. This is a powerful example of the extraordinary value of KM when applied at the global level.

---

34 The Bank for International Settlements. "Trading in foreign exchange markets averaged $5.3 trillion per day in April 2013. This is up from $4.0 trillion in April 2010 and $3.3 trillion in April 2007." The next assessment of the size of foreign exchange markets will take place in 2016.

7. Does our global community make a concerted and sustained effort to encourage and reward people for thinking about, creating and implementing solutions to the greatest issues of our time?

8. Has a global Knowledge Champions Team or KM Community been established? To my knowledge, these do not yet exist—which represents an extremely exciting opportunity! Since global problems require global solutions, a **globally-connected network of KM Communities** would be extraordinarily valuable as a method to collect, assess, store, find, synthesize, leverage and share knowledge collectively at the global scale to help resolve the world community's challenges.

To paint the picture further, the real power of KM lies in our ability to establish KM Communities of all types in all lenses, including communities of practice, communities of interest, communities of purpose, communities of action, amongst others—and then linking these communities together. We'll then be able to share and collaborate and specifically focus on the mission of creating a better world using logic and sound reasoning (KM!) enabled by

the awesome power of the Internet and technology. If we can indeed come together in this
way, tens of millions—even hundreds of millions or billions—of people will be collectively
working towards changing policies, rules, laws
and systems to benefit everyone in the world.

Through this book and *The Power of KM* website (ThePowerofKM.com), we aim to facilitate the creation of this **globally-connected
network of KM Communities**, including the
information and communications technology
(ICT) that will enable easy-to-use communication, sharing and collaboration.

LENS 7: CULTURE/SOCIETY

Culture, as defined by anthropologist Edward Burnett Tylor, is that complex whole which includes
knowledge, belief, art, morals, law, custom and any
other capabilities and habits acquired by man as a
member of society.[35]

The Culture/Society lens gives us a unique way to apply
Knowledge Management to any culture and society. Examples of different cultures and societies include different
tribes, social groups, cities, states, regions and nations.

---

35 *Primitive Culture*, by Edward Burnett Tylor

If we're referring to our *global* culture and society, we could say that this lens encompasses all of the other lenses. However, often when we refer to specific cultures, we're referring to smaller groups of people within the larger global community, in which case the Global Community lens encompasses all of the other lenses.

Some questions to ask are:

1. Are we using Knowledge Management to help shape, inform and guide the way we evolve our society and culture?

2. Does our culture/society make a concerted and sustained effort to encourage and reward people for thinking about, creating and implementing solutions to the greatest issues of our time?

3. Have we established a culture/society Knowledge Champions Team or KM Community? If so, has it been carefully tended to, with adequate communications, awareness, facilitation and support? A **globally-connected network of KM Communities** focused on various cultures

and societies would be extremely useful as a method to collect, assess, store, find, synthesize, leverage and share knowledge collectively at the global scale to help evolve society and culture.

For the most part, the seven lenses are used independently although there can be some overlap. For example, we can deliberately utilize the personal lens with all of the other lenses. Lenses within lenses can also be utilized such as using the project lens in a business environment, which would be using a project lens within a business lens. However, I suggest using these lenses one at a time—at least when starting out with KM—to avoid any unnecessary complexity.

By deliberately choosing which KM lens to use, we can leverage knowledge even more in our efforts to use Knowledge Management to solve problems and increase efficiency, productivity and effectiveness in all areas of our lives.

In the next chapter, we will see how everything you've learned about KM so far comes together using the **Seven Step KM Strategy.**

"It is a simple thing to make things complex, but a complex thing to make things simple."

—ALBERT EINSTEIN

6.

SEVEN STEP KM STRATEGY

The world of Knowledge Management can sometimes feel complicated. The **Seven Step KM Strategy** simplifies the task of implementing KM in our organizations.

In this chapter, you will learn how to combine all of the previously discussed elements to form an easy-to-use, integrated, and universal KM strategy that can be customized and implemented in any environment. We can use the **Seven Step KM Strategy** in a highly customized way, tied back to organizational vision and strategy, to harness the extraordinary value of KM in any organization.

The **Seven Step KM Strategy** consists of the following:

STEP 1: Assess Environment

STEP 2: Survey and Facilitate Existing KM Activities

STEP 3: Plan KM Initiatives

STEP 4: Implement KM Initiatives

STEP 5: Perform Change Management

STEP 6: Implement KM Governance

STEP 7: Socialize, Share and Collaborate

As you can see from the diagram on the next page, following the **Seven Step KM Strategy** starts with Step 1: Assess Environment. The strategy is executed mostly in sequential order, although the double-sided arrows indicate that there can sometimes be some back and forth between steps. In addition, the dotted-line arrows from Step 6 to Step 3 and Step 4 indicate that the process of implementing KM governance involves monitoring and possibly adjusting the actions we're taking in Steps 3 and 4. The same notion applies for the dotted line between Steps 5 and 3; as a result of our change management activities, our plans might need to be updated.

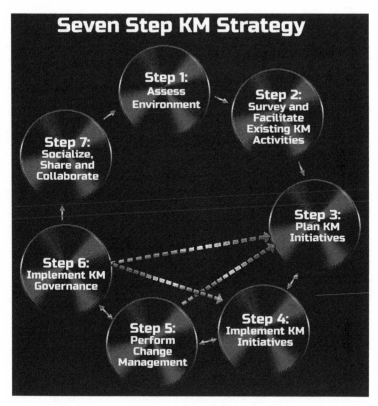

Seven Step KM Strategy

STEP 1: ASSESS ENVIRONMENT

One of the first things to do is determine which of the **Seven Key Lenses of KM** that you will use. Then you must define the *scope* of KM—that is, are you working with a small team, a larger group, or the entire enterprise? Understand the organization's vision, mission, strategy, structure, culture and

SEVEN STEP KM STRATEGY

history, issues, risks and opportunities. This step can also include performing KM audits and assessments to better understand the current state and desired end state. This process will require you to differentiate between everyday knowledge and critical strategic knowledge, with greater priority being given naturally to critical strategic knowledge.

STEP 2: SURVEY AND FACILITATE EXISTING KM ACTIVITIES

Many organizations are performing KM-like functions without even realizing it. A powerful way to help an organization understand the important KM work it is already employing is to conduct a survey to assess any potential KM that is already taking place. Once this knowledge is gathered, help support, facilitate and promote these KM activities, positioning to grow more of them.

STEP 3: PLAN KM INITIATIVES

Based on the information and knowledge uncovered during Steps 1 and 2, carefully design the initiatives to be implemented. Create a custom KM Program that is tied to the organization's vision, mission and strategy. Start by:

1. Creating a prioritized list of potential small, medium and large initiatives that you can carry out within each of the **Seven Key Practice Areas of KM**.

2. Obtain buy-in and support to plan and implement these KM initiatives using the **Seven Key Pillars of KM**.

3. Utilize the **Seven Key Facets of KM** to understand your KM initiatives in an IT-centric manner.

This step also includes the creation of a KM Road Map that shows how to bridge the gap between the current state and the desired end state through KM initiatives.

STEP 4: IMPLEMENT KM INITIATIVES

Implement No-Cost & Low-Cost KM Initiatives

Implementing these kinds of initiatives is also known as creating or succeeding at "quick wins." These can often be run as pilots, which can be expanded to include other parts of the organization later after proving their success. Starting small and attaining success despite a low or even nonexistent budget makes it easier to obtain buy-in for larger initiatives. Success breeds further success.

Implement Larger KM Initiatives

After successfully implementing smaller no-cost and low-cost KM initiatives and socializing these successes, you can then continue to gain more benefits of KM by moving on to larger initiatives. Larger KM initiatives typically require more resources—money, time, people and support from a higher level of management. The success of one medium or large project can help pave the way for even more KM initiatives that produce greater efficiency, productivity, effectiveness and decreased costs.

STEP 5: PERFORM CHANGE MANAGEMENT

Change management is the process of transitioning people, teams and organizations to a desired end state. This helps us deal with the human and organizational dynamics involved with change. It helps us establish various processes—such as strong support and executive sponsorship at a high level, and clear and regular communication about the changes—to ensure that the changes being introduced into the environment take hold and are effective in the long run, effectively ensuring the intended outcomes. By their very nature, many people resist change and need assistance during the transition. Inertia and entrenched habits have a tendency to make even a simple change difficult if the right steps aren't taken to gain support—and help ensure that the desired changes persist in the long run once implemented.

Change management requires ensuring there is high-level support and sponsorship for the changes being introduced, gaining buy-in from stakeholders, ensuring involvement of the right people, dealing with human psychological factors, constant and regular communication about the changes being introduced, consistent and frequent follow-up, reinforcement and removal of obstacles, and recognizing and rewarding those who are involved with the project.

One important dynamic that change management addresses is the fact that change is a process, and it is possible—even likely—for things to get worse before they get better.

The change curve diagram on the next page is based on the work of Swiss-American psychiatrist Elisabeth Kübler-Ross, author of the ground-breaking book *On Death and Dying*.

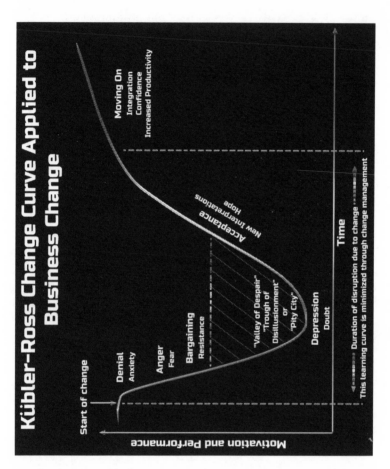

Kübler-Ross Change Curve Applied to Business Change

Kübler-Ross used her book to introduce her theory
of the five stages of grief. In general, people experience most of these stages when faced with their
own imminent death, but the five stages have been
adopted by many as applying to the survivors of a
loved one's death as well.[36]

Kübler-Ross's model can also be utilized for changes
in any organization, and for any type of change that
takes place in our personal lives (job loss, health
problems, loss of a spouse or significant other, etc.)
All of these situations involve major change, and
understanding the dynamics in the change curve can
help us move through these changes more effectively.

As shown in the previous diagram, sometimes people's initial reaction to change is to deny that the
changes are really happening or needed. They think
that perhaps there is a mistake and the changes won't
actually happen. During this stage, people may feel a
sense of anxiety and discomfort.

The next stage in the change curve is feeling a sense
of anger. "Why do we need this change?" or "This

---

36 Wikipedia, "Elisabeth Kübler-Ross"

change is terrible!" or "Why me/us, this isn't fair!". Underlying the feeling of anger is a sense of fear—about what the change means, about the outcome, and fear of how they will move through the process of change, etc.

The next stage is where the person bargains; in the case of learning about having a life-threatening disease, for example, a person might bargain with whatever God the person believes in. When experiencing change in the business world, a person might try to bargain with management to find a way of avoiding undergoing the change. When a person is in this stage, they are basically resisting the change.

After the bargaining stage comes the depression stage. This stage is when a person feels empty, sad, and lacks their normal level of energy and enthusiasm. In this stage, there is doubt about the future in addition to the sadness and depression.

The next stage is acceptance, where the person accepts the change that is taking place. They may not be happy about it, but they accept the situation as it is—which reduces their sense of anxiety, anger, fear, resistance and doubt. They learn to live with the new norm. As a result, they begin feeling a sense of hope and inspiration. New interpretations may come into play, increasing the sense of hope and optimism in the present and in the future.

After the acceptance stage, a person moves on to the new reality. Over time, they integrate their experiences and gain confidence, energy and productivity.

As you can see from the diagram, there is a dotted line across the curve between the Bargaining and Acceptance stages. During this period of time, people might feel a sense of frustration that makes it difficult to quickly see a positive outcome—and may cause them to question or doubt that outcome. This phase is called the "valley of despair," the "trough of disillusionment," or "pity city." Change management helps reduce the duration of this learning curve.

During this sensitive period, it is important to help people focus on what we really want; the outcome of the changes being made. Properly executed change management helps people deal with these changes in a positive manner, where they feel supported. This includes training and helping people recognize and appreciate the sense of loss that can accompany new changes.

There are a number of different change management models used in the business world.[37] It is not within the scope of this book to delve into the details of the various models on change management. However, it is important to pick one or more to use in conjunction with all of your KM initiatives. Change management must be performed frequently and consistently. Even a well-designed KM program is not likely to succeed without proper change management.

STEP 6: IMPLEMENT KM GOVERNANCE

In order to ensure the successful implementation of Knowledge Management, it is important to create a strong and effective governance model. There are different ways to accomplish this—but the two most important parts are to ensure that KM is supported by the highest level of the organization and to create a *governance group*.

---

37 Some of the more common models are the ADKAR Change Management Model, Beckhard and Harris's Change Model, Burke-Litwin's Change Model, David E. Hussey's EASIER Change Model, GE's Change Acceleration Process (CAP), Kotter's 8 Step Change Model, Kübler-Ross's Five Stages Model, Lewin's Change Management Model, McKinsey's 7-S Model, Stephen Covey's 7 Habits Model, Virginia Satir's Change Process, and William Bridge's Transition Model.

A comprehensive enterprise KM program involves every part of the organization, from Human Resources to Operations to Information Technology and beyond. The KM Leader must receive support and respect from the highest level of management.

The most ideal reporting structure would be for the person running the enterprise KM Program—most often called a Chief Knowledge Officer (CKO) or Chief Learning Officer (CLO)—to report directly to the Board of Directors. This helps to ensure the highest level of autonomy and independence, similar to the way some Audit Departments report directly to the Board of Directors. It is more common at this point for the CKO to report to the President/CEO. Some companies choose to have the CKO report to HR, Operations, Information Technology, Marketing, R&D or elsewhere, although these are less than optimal for the reasons stated above.

Most companies just starting KM won't likely have a CKO, but might have someone who is identified as the KM Leader. This person could be Director or VP level. Other potential knowledge worker positions, depending on the size of the company involved, could include:

1. VP/SVP/EVP of Knowledge Management

2. Director of Knowledge Management

3. Knowledge Manager

4. Knowledge Architect

5. Knowledge Librarian

6. Knowledge Engineer

7. Knowledge Specialist

8. Knowledge Analyst

It is vital for the CKO or KM Leader to retain full accountability, responsibility and authority. It is also important to build and sustain broad support and buy-in for the KM Program through proper governance. One way to create a governance group is to create a Knowledge or KM Council, which ensures tight alignment with the needs of the business. The Knowledge Council acts as a steering committee that provides strategic oversight, direction and resources. The Knowledge Champions Team and KM Community, can also play a collaborative role in association with the Knowledge Council. The governance group can also help guide KM policies, procedures, application of best practices, and to participate in the discussion and resolution of different interpretations of knowledge and experience, etc. The Knowledge Council could be composed of a cross-functional team from different areas of the organization and might include Human Relations, Information Technology, and Operations at a minimum.

It is the responsibility of the Knowledge Council to provide as much support as possible to ensure the success of KM initiatives, all while under the leadership of the KM Leader or CKO. The primary role of KM governance is to make sure that KM initiatives are producing effective outcomes. This includes removing challenges or "road blocks" whenever they arise.

STEP 7: SOCIALIZE, SHARE AND COLLABORATE

Successfully implementing KM often involves changing an organization's culture. One important way to gain and build support for KM is to socialize your successes—to tell others about and invite them into your successful KM initiatives. You want to let others know what KM is, how it ties back to the organization's vision, mission and strategy, how you're using it—and of course about successful KM initiatives and the benefits they provide. This is crucial in helping others understand and get onboard with KM's value and importance.

Sharing and collaborating is a very important aspect of KM. The more people are aware of and are practicing KM, the easier it is for it to spread to other parts of the organization and increase the benefits company-wide. Collaborating is a step beyond sharing and cooperating; it requires *consciously working together* to pool resources, share knowledge and information, and benefit from each other's successes. These steps also help encourage the process of transitioning undocumented tacit knowledge into documented explicit knowledge.

The steps in the **Seven Step KM Strategy** are mostly conducted in sequential order, especially the first four steps. However, it is also possible to go back and forth between some of the steps, or to skip steps—keeping in line with the theme that KM can be fluid and non-linear.

For example, an important part of successfully completing Step 4: Implement KM Initiatives is Step 5:

Perform Change Management. Change management is critical in transforming the organization's culture and ensuring that changes being made and KM initiatives being implemented actually *work* in the long term. It's necessary to perform change management during and after implementing successful no-cost and low-cost KM initiatives (the first part of Step 4); we shouldn't wait until we implement larger KM initiatives in Step 4 to perform change management in Step 5.

Similarly, performing change management (Step 5), implementing KM governance (Step 6), and socializing, sharing and collaborating (Step 7) should be conducted *throughout* the process of implementing KM.

In the spirit of moving into action mode and gaining the benefits of KM as quickly as possible, implementing KM governance (Step 6) follows implementing KM initiatives (Step 4) and performing change management (Step 5). However, it is also possible to implement KM governance before implementing KM initiatives in Step 4. What is important about following the Seven Step KM Strategy is to ensure that all steps are eventually completed.

By following the **Seven Step KM Strategy**—and using conversation, dialogue and diplomacy—we can resolve all of our business, personal and global challenges, whatever they may be.

In Chapter 10, you'll see an example walkthrough of the **Seven Step KM Strategy** in action.

Let's now learn about one of the most exciting and important aspects of Knowledge Management: **Wisdom**.

7.

WISDOM

Let's revisit the DIKW Pyramid, first introduced in Chapter 1:

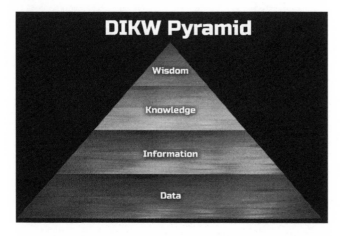

As we can see from the diagram, Wisdom is at the top of the DIKW Pyramid. There are several widely divergent interpretations of what wisdom is in the context of Knowledge Management—and little agreement on the subject.

I have written a highly acclaimed book (now in its 4th edition) on the common ground found within the world's major wisdom traditions. This universal wisdom can be used when thinking about the top level of the DIKW Pyramid. Although that book was not written using the terminology of Knowledge Management, if you wish to learn more about universal wisdom in general—which can be applied in any situation—please refer to *The Rainbow Bridge: Bridge to Inner Peace and to World Peace*.[38]

Since knowledge is understanding gained through experience, what is wisdom? It is difficult to explain or define wisdom, and easier to give examples of wisdom in action. I believe the most important example of wisdom in any environment, including business, is expressed in the following concept:

---

38 *The Rainbow Bridge* has received 22 literary awards and has been endorsed by H.H. the 14th Dalai Lama, New York Times Bestselling Authors, Doctors, Lawyers, Ambassadors, Astronauts, Olympians, an Academy Award-Winning Actor and other prestigious global luminaries.

"Do not do to others what you would not want done to yourself." [39]

In the Information Age, some business people might wonder why words such as these—a variation of the Golden Rule known as the Platinum Rule—has a place in the business world. However, as participants in the Knowledge Age, we are living in a time where knowledge in the business world needs to be infused with wisdom. When we think about wisdom in this light, a few things come to mind, all of which accurately portray various aspects of wisdom. Treating everyone in the workplace with compassion, kindness, patience, respect and dignity is certainly wise. It not only feels good; it also produces the most positive and inspiring outcomes.

We should be guided by our ideals, and attempting to use this rule at all times is deep wisdom. The Platinum Rule applies, for example, when on-boarding and off-boarding new team members, as well as when providing coaching and professional development, including all conversations about job performance.

---

39 As the famous sage and scholar Hillel stated after reciting this quote, "and the rest is commentary." Commentary in the form of conversation, dialogue and diplomacy can be guided by the wisdom-infused use of Knowledge Management.

KM challenges us to use our heads as well as our hearts, to arrive at the most positive and inspiring outcomes possible. As one of my high school teachers used to say when we were performing complex equations, "Put your thinking caps on and keep your wits about you." When we employ calm, level-headed logic and rational thinking in combination with what our hearts tell us, we can truly resolve any of our challenges through conversation, dialogue and diplomacy.

Wisdom and common sense show us that when resolving issues through calm, level-headed conversation, dialogue and diplomacy, common courtesy, civility and decorum are helpful and important. It is not helpful when people are screaming at one another, when people are being insulted or when people are being bullied.

Playing on people's fears and emotions when trying to accomplish something is also not helpful. When people are angry, it is not helpful to stoke the anger; every effort should be made to channel anger or frustration towards a positive outcome. Although it may seem obvious, respect and decorum are very important to the process of resolving issues and creating solutions. These are facts and wisdom that apply in all situations. In a public setting, they are even more important.

When we grasp the concept that everything that can be understood can be known but not everything that can be known can be understood, we move in the direction of deep wisdom. Another mark of wisdom is recognizing that given the near-infinite nature of reality, we actually know very little.

The following diagram shows another way we can understand the progression from data to information to knowledge to wisdom:

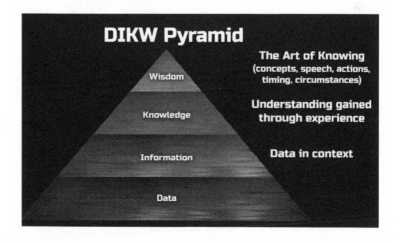

We've learned that knowledge is understanding gained from experience. A step beyond knowledge is wisdom, which is the art of *knowing*. Knowing something goes beyond understanding; it is possible to know something without understanding it. An example of this is the existence of a rainbow. We know that we can see rainbows at certain times but we don't need to realize that a rainbow can only be seen when light is being refracted at a 42-degree angle from the direction opposite the light source.[40] We don't need to understand the science behind rainbows to know that they exist or to witness them.

In addition to knowing a concept, knowing also refers to knowing what to say and what not to say, what to do and what not to do, including when, where and under what circumstances. As humans, this is something that we can always work on and improve.

Another way to understand the progression from data to information to knowledge to wisdom is that data leads to information; information leads to knowledge; knowledge leads to wisdom; and wisdom leads to better decision making and better outcomes—a process shown in the following modified DIKW Pyramid:

---

40 Wikipedia, "rainbow"

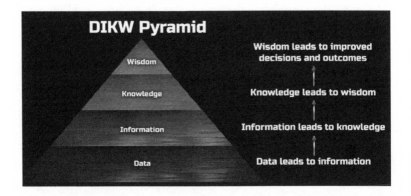

When our KM efforts are guided by and infused with wisdom, they lead to improved decisions with outcomes that are destined for great success.

One way we can see wisdom leading to improved decisions and outcomes is the importance of focusing like a laser on *what we want* as an outcome as opposed to focusing our minds on *what we don't want*. Although this may seem obvious, there are many examples—especially in the world of governmental politics—where officials focus quite a bit on discussing other people, and on matters or situations they're hoping to avoid. It is much more productive and helpful to focus on what we *do* want than on what we don't. Our actions should be driven by a vision of a positive future with a specific outcome as opposed to being driven by fear or by what we don't want.

For example, rather than spending our time thinking about the customers who aren't buying our products or services, spend time thinking of the new customers who *will* be buying once they hear about us, or thinking about how to keep our existing customers satisfied. Rather than focusing on the investment capital we don't have, focus on who will be thrilled to invest and exactly what we will do with the funds once we receive the investment. Focus on the desired outcome rather than the existing challenges. Yes, it's important to have a plan for these challenges; but concentrating on what we want as opposed to what we *don't* want will help us expend our energy in the right places.

Another way we can see how wisdom leads to better decisions and outcomes is addressing *root causes* despite the challenges that might arise. Let's take a look at an example from our governmental institutions.

One of the greatest global issues of our time is terrorism. The root cause of terrorism is poverty, which gives rise to anger and lack of hope, which in turn gives rise to extreme views and interpretations—religious

THE POWER OF KM

and otherwise. Rather than focusing on terrorists—
and imagining what they might do, or fixating on our
fear or the images we see in the media—we should
spend our time and energy focusing primarily on
addressing the root cause of poverty.

Of course, determining how to address the root
cause of poverty worldwide is complex and daunt-
ing for many people. So instead, they reject the idea
entirely and focus on something else more immediate such as killing the terrorists. Anyone who would
harm an innocent person must be stopped, that's for
sure. But if we're not careful how we use our minds,
we can get lost in our thoughts and forget that we
will go around in circles until we address the root
cause of any issue or challenge. This is not only logical but is deep wisdom in any situation.

Another example of how wisdom in business leads to
better decisions and outcomes is the rapidly growing
interest and application of corporate social responsibility (CSR), also known as conscious capitalism or
corporate citizenship. This wise approach to running
companies is based on the fact that everything is
interconnected and that organizations do not operate

in a vacuum. This evolved approach to business rec-
ognizes that in order for businesses to be optimally
effective and long-lasting, they need to take good
care of their employees, partners, customers and the
communities in which they operate and serve with the
highest degree of dignity, transparency and respect.
The top five companies in the world based on CSR
ratings in 2015 are (1) Google, (2) BMW, (3) The Walt
Disney Company, (4) Microsoft and (5) Daimler.[41]

To provide a few examples of what some of these
companies are doing to receive high CSR ratings,
50% of all energy consumption at BMW is driven
by renewable energy.[42] In addition, BMW is using a
wind turbine to power the factory that makes its i-3
electric car.[43]

Google has been carbon neutral since 2007, invested
in energy-reduction programs in its data centers
(which the company says use half the energy of
comparable centers), and it's agreed to fund $2 bil-
lion in renewable energy projects. Google has also

41 Reputation Institute's 2015 Global CSR RepTrak® 100 Report
42 Reputation Institute's 2015 Global CSR RepTrak® 100 Report
43 Forbes Magazine, "The Companies with the Best CSR Reputations in the
World," September 17, 2015

promised to increase diversity, setting goals to hire more women and people of color.[44]

In the United States, a benefit corporation is a type of for-profit corporate entity, legislated in 28 U.S. states, that includes positive impact on society and the environment in addition to profit as its legally defined goals. The purpose of a benefit corporation includes creating general public benefit, which is defined as a material positive impact on society and the environment. A benefit corporation's directors and officers operate the business with the same authority as in a traditional corporation but are required to consider the impact of their decisions not only on shareholders, but also on society and the environment. In a traditional corporation, shareholders judge the company's financial performance; with a benefit corporation, shareholders judge performance based on how a corporation's goals benefit society and the environment.[45]

Benefit corporations differ from traditional corporations in purpose, accountability, and transparency, but not in taxation. The rise of social responsibility

44 Forbes Magazine, "The Companies with the Best CSR Reputations in the World," September 17, 2015
45 Wikipedia, "Benefit corporation"

in business and the creation of benefit corporations—which are being adopted internationally—are a demonstration of wisdom in action. Some examples of benefit corporations include Ben and Jerry's, Kickstarter, Patagonia, Change.org, Etsy, Hootsuite, The Honest Company, Seventh Generation, Method, Warby Parker, Plum Organics, Farmigo, King Arthur Flour, Klean Kanteen, Natura, Cooperative Home Care Associates, Cascade Engineering, Solberg Manufacturing, Evox Television and Triodos Bank.

We've already discussed some ways we can use KM in our personal lives—the importance of which is brought to light in one of the most important reminders of wisdom, a message inscribed on The Temple of Apollo at Delphi:

"Temet Nosce"

—LATIN, for "Know Thyself"

It is not only important for *individuals* to know themselves; organizations and institutions should strive to do the same. It would be wise to apply this wisdom by becoming more introspective and learning more about why we make the decisions we make, and to ultimately make better decisions through the use of Knowledge Management. A few questions that can help businesses as they turn inward are:

1. Who are we as a company, what do we stand for? What values do we espouse?

2. Why are we here?

3. How much and in what ways do we care about our employees?

4. How much and in what ways do we care about our customers?

5. How much and in what ways do we care about the lives of the people who live in the communities in which we serve and operate?

6. Do we serve a cause that is bigger than our own company?

Another crucial point to wisdom is that although there is a mental aspect, most of it is heart-based. Having patience, kindness, compassion, and giving others the benefit of the doubt are examples of heart-based wisdom in action. So rather than focusing on what divides us when working with others, it is wise and helpful to focus on common ground—what we share and what brings us together. When people and teams feel a sense of togetherness, of being included rather than excluded, they tend to be more satisfied, productive and stay with companies longer.

It is also wise to recognize and appreciate the fact that knowledge *evolves*—something that's not only natural, but to be expected. Innovation and creativity help evolve knowledge, as do experiences—since knowledge is understanding gained through experience. Access to new information evolves knowledge, since what we know as facts today may be known tomorrow as misunderstandings or errors.

For example, up until the late 16th century, everyone "knew" that the sun and planets revolved around the Earth. That understanding was later proven to be false.[46] Another example that demonstrates the evolution of knowledge is up until the late 19th century, doctors "knew" that the best way to help people with serious illnesses was to drain their blood, sometimes with leeches.[47] Fortunately, modern science

---

46 Wikipedia, "Heliocentrism"
47 Wikipedia, "Bloodletting"

and medicine now have much more advanced ways to help heal diseases. We should not be disturbed by the impermanent nature of knowledge, but rather, be excited and inspired by it.

It is common for everyone to occasionally take certain things—even knowledge itself—for granted. For example, it was only in the mid 1800's that medical doctors gained the knowledge of how to administer anesthesia. Prior to that time, many medical procedures were horrific, with no way to reduce or eliminate extreme pain and agony. Amputations and other serious medical procedures had to be done with the patient laying on a table, with the injured person biting on a piece of wood to stop from screaming. Knowledge provides value beyond the date in which it was first discovered. It is wise to understand and appreciate knowledge, whenever it was first discovered, as knowledge is powerful, long-lasting and extraordinarily valuable. As 12th century French philosopher Bernard of Chartres expressed, "we truly stand on the shoulders of the giants who have come before us."

It's also wise to recognize that everything is not always as it appears; situations, experiences and life itself can be like an illusion. How often have you had a thought about something, only to find out later that it wasn't anything at all like you had imagined? For example, have you ever been called into your boss's office and immediately felt like you were in trouble— only to find out that he or she wanted to give you praise or an exciting new assignment?

We've all had experiences that we can relate to where we essentially rushed to judgment, and that judgment later turned out to be false. It requires deep wisdom to make judgments only once gathering the *current*, *accurate* and *complete* facts and knowledge—even if it takes more time. Although it may seem obvious, this means that it is extremely important to not forget, discount or discard history.

A related example of wisdom is the concept of making a conscious decision to not miss out on a blessing because it might not be packaged the way you would expect. An example of this is when hiring new team members who might dress, look or talk differently than you think they should, a knee-jerk reaction might be to reject the person because you think "they won't fit in." You could very well miss out on hiring an amazingly talented person to join your team. If you reject them based on appearances alone, you may well be letting a huge asset walk out the door—because it's not packaged the way you would normally expect.

As we know, Knowledge Management aims to maximize human capital; therefore, KM is **all** about people. It is deep wisdom to remember this at all times when making decisions, just as it is wise for us to constantly keep in mind and apply the Platinum Rule. It is deep wisdom to recognize that when we take care of our people, our people will take care of us and our organization.

8.

A VISION FOR THE FUTURE OF KM

WISDOM-INFUSED KNOWLEDGE

I see a very bright future for Knowledge Management during the current transition from the Information Age to the Knowledge Age. During the Information Age, decisions were made largely through the use of data and information. In the Knowledge Age, people are making better decisions by using wisdom-infused knowledge.

KM BECOMES MAINSTREAM

As more people and organizations learn about the power and benefits of KM, what may seem like exciting and novel ways of maximizing knowledge and human capital will become the norm, only to be replaced by even *more* creative and innovative ideas. Companies that leverage KM will see improved efficiency, productivity and effectiveness, as well as creative innovations in their products and services— and companies that fail to embrace Knowledge Management will lose opportunities to those that do.

ELEVATED PRIORITY OF CONTINUOUS LEARNING

I see a future where companies become even more committed to helping their employees grow continuously through extensive professional development and training programs. Performing lessons learned before, during and after major events or projects will become commonplace and expected, as it makes sense and provides solid value.

CONTINUOUS IMPROVEMENT THROUGH BEST PRACTICES AND INNOVATION

Operating in the spirit of continuous improvement, successful organizations will regularly research and promote best practices that result in increased efficiency and productivity. Creativity and innovation will be increasingly encouraged and rewarded, prompting the flow of creative useful ideas to increase. This will be true both inside and outside our organizations in the form of innovative products and services we offer to our customers.

METRICS TO ENSURE SUCCESS

While we must accept that not everything that has value can be accurately measured, creative ways of utilizing metrics will be developed and widely shared, allowing KM practitioners to fine tune their efforts and determine what's working versus what they need to improve. Through case studies, powerful examples of cost savings and high ROI will inspire companies to invest even more heavily in KM, leading to yet more innovative and creative ideas, solutions and benefits.

RENEWED APPRECIATION FOR KNOWLEDGE

Engagement of employees and team members through Knowledge Management will grow. The formation of Knowledge Councils will help guide KM activities and initiatives. People from different parts of the organization will each contribute and learn from one another, demonstrating a renewed appreciation for knowledge, teamwork, sharing and collaboration.

ON-BOARDING, OFF-BOARDING, LESSONS LEARNED, BEST PRACTICES AND OTHER KM INITIATIVES

To optimize knowledge transfer and maximize use of knowledge, organizations will regularly perform well-planned on-boarding and off-boarding when new team members join and others move on. They will implement Lessons Learned processes consistently and share best practices as a standard and expected way of operating. KM initiatives will be discussed and celebrated in board rooms and conference rooms in organizations across the world and receive high-level support—because it is an approach that makes sense and produces extraordinary value.

DEVELOPMENT OF POWERFUL NEW SYSTEMS

Companies will create powerful software to enable easy-to-use, effective search capabilities, giving rise to a new generation of knowledge repositories. These systems shall ensure that the right knowledge is easily available to the right person at the right time.

INFUSION OF WISDOM INTO THE BUSINESS WORLD

The professional discipline of Knowledge Management will open the door for discussing and appreciating wisdom in the business world. It will lead to an increased awareness that everything is connected, and that we all gain when we work together to share, learn and grow. We'll also become even more conscious of how to use Knowledge Management in virtually every area of our lives, in all of our companies, organizations and institutions worldwide.

THE RISE OF BENEFIT CORPORATIONS

There will be increased awareness and appreciation for Benefit corporations. Many companies will restructure to demonstrate their commitment to doing business in a better, more socially responsible manner while still making a handsome profit.

SOLVING PROBLEMS USING KM, CONVERSATION, DIALOGUE AND DIPLOMACY

There will be widespread recognition of the power and extraordinary value of implementing Knowledge Management with level-headed conversation, dialogue and diplomacy to resolve our challenges, whatever they may be.

THE ADVENT OF A GLOBALLY-CONNECTED NETWORK OF KM COMMUNITIES

Nonprofit, social profit and Benefit corporations will begin to form mutually-beneficial alliances. There will be a **globally-linked network of KM Communities** enabled by the Internet that will allow organizations to collectively share knowledge and collaborate in ways that provide unprecedented value and opportunity. These KM Communities of all types, in all lenses—including communities of practice, interest, purpose, and action, amongst others—are linked together. We'll then be able to collectively share and collaborate with the mission of creating a better world using logic and sound reasoning enabled by technology. If we can indeed come together in this way, tens of millions—even hundreds of millions or billions—of people will be collectively working towards changing policies, rules, laws and systems to benefit everyone in the world.

KM IMPROVES THE QUALITY OF LIFE WORLDWIDE

There will be increased awareness that global problems require global solutions, and that the power of KM allows us to come together to resolve all of our seemingly intractable challenges. KM will bring about exciting new developments that improve the quality of life for billions of people worldwide.

In the next chapter, you will be inspired by the **KM Call to Action**.

9.

CALL TO ACTION

THE WORLD NEEDS KM

We truly stand at the dawn of a new era in the Knowledge Age. We are faced with an alarmingly large number of simultaneous global challenges, and yet we have an enormous opportunity to come together to do things differently than we have in the past. The fact that we are faced with multiple simultaneous crises is actually an enormous opportunity, for if there was ever a time when we need to come together in a global, concerted, unified fashion, that time is now.

Every person and organization can benefit through the optimized use of knowledge available to them. One could even say that those who know about KM have a responsibility to use it—not only to improve their own lives—but also the lives of billions of people worldwide. Special times call for special measures, and KM can help make a significant shift in the trajectory the world is headed.

PERSONAL KM

By utilizing the Personal lens of KM, we can live happy, successful, productive and amazing lives with a sense of inner harmony and fulfillment. The more peaceful and collected we are in our personal lives, the more effective and successful we are in our work lives. Therefore, Knowledge workers practicing personal KM are even more effective and successful with their organizational KM initiatives. Personal KM is a powerful tool personally and professionally, and we owe it to ourselves to take advantage of it.

KM IN EVERY ORGANIZATION WORLDWIDE

As you know, KM is all about optimizing the use of human capital. Since every organization has people—human capital, every organization in the world has the opportunity to harness the extraordinary value of KM. As we've seen throughout the book, this is true for businesses, nonprofit organizations, religious/spiritual organizations, clubs, non-governmental organizations, governmental agencies, militaries and at the highest levels of national and global leadership. Every organization in the world should consider the use of KM to not only improve themselves internally, but also to make a difference in the world around them.

TOP-DOWN KM

Fully optimized KM requires the strong support of top leadership in an organization. KM can indeed be successful without support from the top but it's much more challenging and requires more time to be successful. Without top-down support, it's not possible to implement the most effective KM across the entire enterprise in an integrated, holistic fashion.

Top-down support for KM requires constant communication about KM in general, KM initiatives and the value they bring. Continuous communication, promotion and marketing of KM ensure a high degree of internal company visibility. An organization's top leadership must also provide quick and effective removal of any roadblocks that may arise, and is well-served to provide the adequate level of resources for all KM initiatives and for the KM Program overall.

BOTTOM-UP/GRASSROOTS KM

Bottom-up or grassroots KM can take place in an organization as a way to spread awareness about KM and to demonstrate the extraordinary value of KM, often with a very limited budget or no budget at all. In an organization without strong support for KM at the top of the organization, there is no need to wait to implement it in a bottom-up grassroots manner.

It is important to focus in a targeted manner where you have maximum opportunity to be successful. Start with small projects or initiatives. Achieve success and show the value of KM, and expand KM from that point. Pilots are very important and allow for the opportunity of conducting a shared Lessons Learned in the spirit of continuous improvement.

You can create a Buddy Program relatively easily and quickly, and can create a Knowledge Champions Team even more quickly. And every organization can create a document or repository that describes common policies, processes, procedures, systems, contacts, etc.

Eventually, you can create a KM Community, with the goal of eventually having an enterprise KM

Community that shares best practices, knowledge, experiences, KM initiatives, lessons learned, and more. Organizations of all types can use the KM Roadmap in Chapter 10 as a powerful way to start to their KM efforts.

BRIDGE-BUILDING KM

People who use calm, level-headed conversation, dialogue and diplomacy to advance the cause of Knowledge Management are bridge-builders. Each person bridges ideas and concepts through their hearts and minds, guided by the use of wisdom-infused knowledge and Knowledge Management.

Top-down KM requires support and feeding, and naturally requires the support of top leaders. Anyone who is leading support for KM from the top needs to work with those lower in the organization. They are also a bridge to the lower rungs of the organization, and are therefore bridge-builders performing bridge-building KM.

Similarly, if the attempted use of KM is not yet receiving the full understanding or support of top leadership in your organization, it is again the bottom-up grassroots people who can help build bridges to leadership and laterally to their peers through wisdom-infused KM. You do not have to wait to receive support from top management to continue moving KM forward in an organization, including when applying it at the global level.

GLOBAL NETWORK OF KM COMMUNITIES

You have seen that it is of great value to create a Knowledge Champions Team and KM Community in our organizations. These actions alone will provide great value. Similar to how it makes sense to share knowledge across an enterprise in the spirit of learning and benefiting from one another, imagine the value when organizations around the world come together in the same fashion.

Imagine millions of organizations around the world using KM. Imagine the value and opportunities we could generate by coming together through a **globally-connected network of KM Communities** that are guided by the use of wisdom-infused KM.

An untapped and extraordinary value of KM lies in our ability to establish KM Communities of all types in all lenses, including communities of practice, communities of interest, communities of purpose, communities of action, amongst others—and then linking these communities together using the Internet. We would be able to collaborate with the shared mission of creating a better world using wisdom-infused KM, conversation, dialogue and diplomacy. If we can indeed come together in this way, tens of millions—even hundreds of millions or billions—of people will be collectively working towards changing policies, rules, laws and systems to benefit everyone in the world. To join our **globally-connected network of KM Communities**, please visit us at The-PowerofKM.com.

In the next chapter, we will walk through the **Seven Step KM Strategy** using a fictitious company to underscore and clarify how the strategy works.

10.

SEVEN STEP KM STRATEGY
EXAMPLE WALKTHROUGH

Let's now walk through the **Seven Step KM Strategy** using a fictitious company, ABC123 Software, as an example. ABC123 is a software development company that specializes in website and mobile application development, has 100 employees, has been in operation for seven years and is experiencing rapid growth. The CEO recently heard about *The Power of KM* through a friend who said he should read it—and is now eager to leverage the power of KM at his company.

Please note that this example can also be used to start and expand KM in a company or organization of any size. For example, a company of 5,000 people could have a few different teams, each implementing a KM Program similar to the one discussed in this chapter, in different divisions, with each division being comprised of 100 or more people. In such an example, the company is well positioned to eventually run their KM Program at the enterprise level. The KM initiatives taking place at lower levels in the company are run as pilots and pave the way for larger KM initiatives at the enterprise level. This is an example of how the seeds of KM can be planted and grown at the grassroots level without support from upper management, if necessary.

We learned back in Chapter 6 about the **Seven Step KM Strategy** for implementing successful KM:

STEP 1: Assess Environment

STEP 2: Survey and Facilitate Existing KM Activities

STEP 3: Plan KM Initiatives

STEP 4: Implement KM Initiatives

STEP 5: Perform Change Management

STEP 6: Implement KM Governance

STEP 7: Socialize, Share and Collaborate

Let us now walk through the **Seven Step KM Strategy** at ABC123 Software.

STEP 1: ASSESS ENVIRONMENT

One of the first things to do is determine which of the **Seven Key Lenses of KM** that we will use. For this example, we will use the **KM in Business Lens**.

After we study to ensure that we understand the company or team's vision, mission and strategy, we endeavor to understand the company's or team's issues, risks and opportunities. ABC123's mission is to develop powerful, easy to use software, with a focus on website and mobile application development. With this small company of 100 team members, we decide to skip performing formal KM audits and assessments at this time, knowing that following the Seven Step KM Strategy includes an initial assessment of our environment.

STEP 2: SURVEY AND FACILITATE EXISTING KM ACTIVITIES

As a result of a quick survey, we learn that a few teams have developed their own versions of a paper-based "Operations Guide" to document key processes, procedures, org charts, key contact names and numbers. These tools are aimed at helping new team members come up to speed and reducing the learning curve. The managers of the teams using these tools feel they are invaluable at accelerating new team members' learning curves. Because of how powerful a tool these have proven to be, the ABC123 CEO supports a low-cost initiative to come up with a single, consistent document and spread this best practice to the entire organization. There are also discussions underway about transitioning from a paper-based system to an online solution. Although no one was aware of it, they were already implementing KM!

STEP 3: PLAN KM INITIATIVES

Based on the information and knowledge uncovered above, we are ready to design our KM initiatives. We create a custom KM Program that is tied to our organization's vision, mission and strategy of developing software. We start by:

1. Creating a prioritized list of potential small, medium and large initiatives that can be carried out within each of the **Seven Key Practice Areas of KM**. We decide to implement the following KM initiatives:

    1. Implement paper-based Operations Guide across the company (small)

2. Implement a company Buddy Program (small)

3. Execute team-building activities such as a monthly offsite lunch and administering the Myers-Briggs Type Indicator (small)

4. Encourage knowledge sharing and team-work by adding to performance appraisal expectations (small)

5. Launch and cultivate a company KM Community (medium)

6. Implement off-boarding process to capture and leverage knowledge through exit interviews (medium)

7. Develop a Lessons Learned Management System to facilitate the learning of lessons before, during and after key events, projects or milestones (medium)

8. Migrate paper-based company Operations Guide to web space (medium)

9. Start planning to develop company knowledge repository (large, in the future)

2. Obtain buy-in and support to plan and implement these KM initiatives using the **Seven Key Pillars of KM**.

As we learned about in Chapter 4, here are the **Seven Key Pillars of Knowledge Management**:

1. Reduce Knowledge Discovery Time

2. Improve Knowledge Processes

3. Foster Knowledge-Based Teamwork

4. Integrate / Leverage New Knowledge

5. Collaborate / Share Knowledge

6. Manage Knowledge Risks

7. Promote 3-Way Enterprise Knowledge

Although we already have a list of KM initiatives we would like to implement, it's still important to go through each of the seven key pillars, asking ourselves key questions that can help uncover additional opportunities. Remember, it is perfectly fine if some initiatives span across multiple pillars; in fact, this is a sign of a particularly impactful KM initiative.

Let us now go through questions related to the **Seven Key Pillars of KM**.

Pillar 1: Reduce Knowledge Discovery Time

Some questions to ask ourselves when reducing knowledge discovery and rediscovery time include:

1. Do we provide new team members with on-boarding and knowledge transfer resources such as Operations Manuals, Resource Guides, Welcome Packets or websites that allow them to get started on doing their actual jobs—instead of needing to spend a great deal of time learning the ropes?

2. Do we have an internal corporate Knowledge Base (KB) where team members can find key knowledge about the company—things like organization charts, organizational charters, information about company benefits, policies, procedures, self-service customer support, answers to commonly asked questions, etc.? If so, is it updated regularly and by whom?

3. Do we perform a Lessons Learned process before, during and after major events

or projects/initiatives are completed? Do we make it easy for others to search through this knowledge so they can benefit from what others have already learned?

We already decided to implement a paper-based Operations Guide across ABC123 Software, and then to migrate this to a web space. We also decided to develop a Lessons Learned Management System and to start planning a company knowledge repository. Therefore, the following KM initiatives belong within Pillar 1:

Pillar 1

Reduce Knowledge Discovery Time

- Implement paper-based Operations Guide across the company (yr 1)

- Migrate company paper-based Operations Guide to web (yr 1)

- Develop Lessons Learned Management System (yr 2)

- Start planning company knowledge repository (yr 2)

Pillar 2: Improve Knowledge Processes
Some questions to ask when improving knowledge processes include:

1. Are we using any processes that could be improved?

2. What mechanisms are we using to seek out and reward suggestions for making our processes better and more efficient, in the spirit of continuous improvement in our organization?

We already decided to encourage knowledge sharing and teamwork by adding this to the performance appraisal criteria, and to implement an off-boarding process that includes capturing and leveraging knowledge through exit interviews.

As a result of asking ourselves the above questions, we notice that we have an opportunity at ABC123 to create a company Innovation Award and decide to add it to our plans. We decide to create a simple award program: once a year to reward the first, second and third most innovative ideas submitted. We decide to keep the cost down and to award $100 for first place, $75 for second place and $50 for third place, in addition to the winners being given a framed certificate. All of these KM initiatives belong within Pillar 2:

Pillar 2

Improve Knowledge Processes

- Implement Innovation Awards Program (yr 1)

- Update performance appraisal criteria (yr 1)

- Implement off-boarding process with exit interviews (yr 2)

Pillar 3: Foster Knowledge-Based Teamwork

Some questions to ask when fostering knowledge-based teamwork include:

1. Do we have an official or unofficial "Buddy Program" where new team members are encouraged to pair up with an existing team member? Buddy Programs help create ways for increasing knowledge transfer and that strengthen relationships. At ABC123, this program would be especially helpful because of the many software development processes, procedures and standards that new team members are expected to adhere to. Being able to seek informal guidance and assistance from a buddy in addition to their manager is a great way to share knowledge and helps build team spirit.

2. Do we have regular team-building programs, offsite outings, etc.?

3. Do we have any programs that encourage sharing of knowledge about each other? For example, some organizations have a "featured employee" section on their website or in their newsletters, etc.

4. Do we have programs that encourage understanding ourselves and others such as Myers-Briggs, DISC and StrengthsFinder, among others (please refer to Chapter 3: Seven Key Practice Areas of KM for more examples)? Such programs increase our sensitivity and understanding of ourselves and others, minimize friction between people and teams, and help our teams and organizations to be more effective.

5. Do we have any programs that encourage and reward innovation?

6. Do we have a Knowledge Champions Team or a KM Community?

We already decided to implement a company Buddy Program, to offer periodic team-building activities, to encourage knowledge sharing and teamwork by adding this to the performance appraisal criteria and to create a KM Community to further the cause of KM at ABC123. However, we had forgotten about creating a Knowledge Champions Team and decide to add it to our plans. All of these KM initiatives belong within Pillar 3:

- Create a Knowledge Champions Team (yr 1)
- Implement company Buddy Program (yr 1)
- Offer periodic team-building activities (yr 1)
- Update performance appraisal criteria (yr 1)
- Create a KM Community (yr 1)

Pillar 4: Integrate / Leverage New Knowledge

Some questions to ask when integrating/leveraging new knowledge include:

1. Do we have programs or initiatives that encourage continual learning, especially when

paired with encouragement and support to utilize this new knowledge?

2. Do we have programs or initiatives that encourage and reward innovation and creativity, even if it means there may be occasional failures?

We already decided to implement a company Innovation Awards Program at ABC123, which we included in Pillar 2, and Knowledge Champions Team and KM Community in Pillar 3. Let's also encourage continual learning by offering each employee up to $1000 worth of training and professional development per year. All of these KM initiatives belong within Pillar 4:

Pillar 4

Integrate / Leverage New Knowledge

• Implement company Innovation Awards Program (yr 1)

• Create a Knowledge Champions Team and KM Community (yr 1)

• Encourage continual learning by offering training & professional development (yr 2-3)

Pillar 5: Collaborate / Share Knowledge

Some questions to ask when collaborating/sharing knowledge include:

1. Are we enthusiastically and deliberately sharing our knowledge with other people and teams, inside and outside of our own company or organization?

2. Do we have an active and intentional program that encourages collaboration with other people and organizations?

3. If we are actively sharing knowledge with other people and teams, what methods do we use? Can we increase sharing through other means?

4. Do we encourage the use of best practices?

5. Do we have a "Brown Bag" program where knowledge is shared, casually over lunch, in person and/or online?

We already decided to develop a Lessons Learned Management System and to start planning a company knowledge repository, which we included in Pillar 1. In addition, we decided to implement a company

KM Community in Pillars 3 and 4. All of these KM initiatives belong within Pillar 5:

- Create a Knowledge Champions Team and KM Community (yr 1)

- Implement a Buddy Program (yr 1)

- Develop Lessons Learned Management System (yr 2)

- Start planning company knowledge repository (yr 2)

Pillar 6: Manage Knowledge Risks

Some questions to ask when managing knowledge risks include:

1. Do we have a significant number of people who will soon retire? If so, what is our plan to ensure that we don't lose these team members' valuable knowledge when they leave?

2. Do we have a significant number of people in one part of our organization that will soon be downsized? If so, what are we doing to keep these team members' valuable knowledge in

house? Do we have a plan to help these people find other positions in our company?

3. Do we have gaps of knowledge in our environment? For example, if our organization creates proposals to generate new business, do we have all of the knowledge we need to create the best possible proposal?

4. In general, does our organization share knowledge or do they keep it to themselves? If we're using KM at the project level, do we have team members that are not sharing their knowledge?

5. Do we have effective on-boarding and off-boarding programs, including capturing knowledge via exit interviews? Without capturing knowledge via exit interviews, valuable knowledge literally walks out the door.

We already decided to develop a Lessons Learned Management System and to start planning a company knowledge repository, which we included in other pillars. In addition, we decided to implement an off-boarding process to capture and leverage knowledge through exit interviews, which we included in Pillar 2. All of these KM initiatives belong within Pillar 6:

Pillar 6

Manage Knowledge Risks

- Implement off-boarding process with exit interviews (yr 2)

- Develop Lessons Learned Management System (yr 2)

- Start planning company knowledge repository (yr 2)

Pillar 7: Promote 3-Way Enterprise Knowledge

Some questions we can ask when promoting enterprise knowledge include:

1. Is enterprise-wide knowledge shared effectively from the top of the organization down? Are processes, standards, regulations, and best practices easily accessible and widely known?

2. Do we encourage people and teams to share innovative and useful ideas upwards and laterally in the organization to share across the enterprise?

3. Do we regularly conduct Lessons Learned sessions before, during and after major events, projects or milestones, to collect and share this knowledge for the benefit of other people and

teams? If so, are others aware of this resource? What do we do with the knowledge once it is captured? Is it easily searchable by others so they too can benefit?

We already decided to implement a paper-based Operations Guide across the company and to move it to the web. We also decided to develop a Lessons Learned Management System and to start planning a company knowledge repository, which we included in other pillars. All of these KM initiatives belong within Pillar 7:

Pillar 7

Promote 3-Way Enterprise Knowledge

- Implement paper-based Operations Guide across the company (yr 1)

- Migrate company paper-based Operations Guide to web (yr 1)

- Develop Lessons Learned Management System (yr 2)

- Start planning company knowledge repository (yr 2)

We have now identified a series of exciting KM initiatives and assigned them to the **Seven Key Pillars of KM**. Please refer to the following diagrams:

- **Page 186:** view all of the ABC123 KM initiatives on one page, pillar by pillar.

- **Page 187:** view all of the ABC123 KM initiatives on one page, pillar by pillar, with color-coded status for each pillar (red, yellow or green shown in black and white in this book).

- **Page 188:** view all of the ABC123 KM initiatives on one page, pillar by pillar, with color-coded status for each pillar and for each initiative (red, yellow or green shown in black and white in this book).

- **Page 189:** a KM road map that shows each of the ABC123 KM initiatives mapped out across a 3-year period of time.

Sample Initiatives by Seven Key Pillars of KM

Sample Initiatives by Seven Key Pillars of KM
with Status Indicator for Each Pillar

Sample Initiatives by Seven Key Pillars of KM with Status Indicator for Each Pillar and Initiative

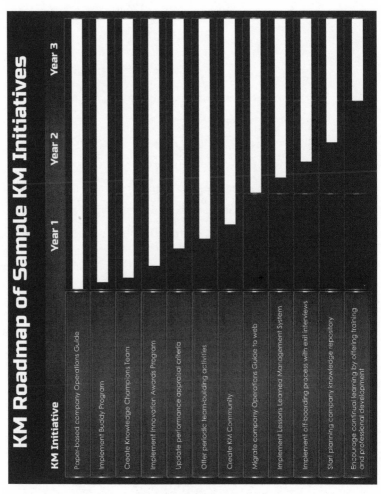

KM Roadmap

STEP 4: IMPLEMENT KM INITIATIVES

Implement No-Cost & Low-Cost KM Initiatives

This step involves implementing the no-cost and low-cost KM initiatives you planned during the previous steps. By successfully implementing quick wins and harvesting the low-hanging fruit (such as creating the Buddy Program, Knowledge Champions Team, Innovation Awards Program and team-building activities), you pave the way for success with larger KM initiatives. Starting small and proving our initiatives to be successful despite no budget or a low budget will make it easier to obtain buy-in and support for larger initiatives.

Implement Larger KM Initiatives

After implementing the previously-mentioned quick wins and socializing their successes, we gain even more benefits of KM by moving on to larger initiatives. The success of one medium or large project can help pave the way for even more KM initiatives that produce greater efficiency, productivity, effectiveness and decreased costs.

STEP 5: PERFORM CHANGE MANAGEMENT

It is important to be persistent in not only the KM initiatives, but with change management to help people adjust to change. Understand and appreciate the human dynamic when dealing with change. Help reduce the learning curve and support people by providing clear and constant communication about the KM initiatives and the desired end state. Ensure there is high-level support for KM and for all of your KM initiatives.

Gain buy-in from stakeholders, and involve the right people and teams. Whenever you experience an obstacle or roadblock, remove them regularly and frequently. Recognize and reward those who are involved with the sharing and implementation of KM on a regular basis.

Perform change management diligently throughout all steps of the Seven Step KM Strategy. Since the CEO is the driving force behind implementing KM at ABC123 Software, there is support at the highest level so change management will be easier than it otherwise might be.

STEP 6: IMPLEMENT KM GOVERNANCE

For our example of implementing KM at ABC123 Software, we decide to keep our KM governance structure simple, agile and flexible. After we enlist the support of high-level management, we decide that the person leading the charge on the KM program is called the KM Leader.

The KM Leader spearheads the creation of a Knowledge Council, which is comprised of people from various parts of the organization as discussed in Chapter 6, Step 6. The Knowledge Council ensures tight alignment with the needs of the business, and acts as a steering committee that helps provide strategic oversight, direction and resources. Once it is launched, the ABC123 Software Knowledge Champions Team and KM Community are invited to play a collaborative role in association with the Knowledge Council.

It is helpful to remember that the primary role of KM governance is to make sure that our KM initiatives are producing effective outcomes. This includes removing challenges or "road blocks" whenever they arise. Since ABC123 Software receives strong support directly from the CEO, challenges and road blocks are quickly removed and before long, ABC123 begins to harness the extraordinary value of Knowledge Management.

STEP 7: SOCIALIZE, SHARE AND COLLABORATE

As your KM initiatives take hold and become successful, talk to others and share the good news. This is not only an opportunity to announce the initiatives' success and benefits and invite others into them; it is also an opportunity to share your knowledge about KM with others, and helping them understand the value and importance of KM.

As we know, sharing and collaborating is a very important part of KM. The more people are aware of and are practicing KM, the easier it is for it to spread to other parts of the organization. Share and deliberately collaborate as much as possible. Together you are all stronger and more likely to experience success in all of your KM initiatives. ABC123 Software conducts regular brown bag sessions to share the status and plans of KM initiatives in its enterprise KM Program.

•   •   •

To receive professional consulting regarding implementing KM in your organization, please visit our collaborative network in development at ThePowerofKM.com where we have started to create a KM Community. It's a great way to connect to a community of people who are embarking on the same journey of implementing Knowledge Management as you are. Join us to facilitate the creation of a **globally-connected network of KM Communities** to collectively harness the extraordinary value of KM in the Knowledge Age and to help make the world a better place than we found it.

ABOUT THE AUTHOR

 With two graduate degrees and eleven professional certifications in Knowledge Management, Change Management, Project Management, Quality, and Agile Methodology, Brent Hunter is the author of five books, an IT professional, producer, former psychotherapist and National Certified Counselor. He has held many positions ranging from a software engineer experienced in ten programming languages, to Systems Analyst, Project Manager, Technology Manager, and CIO/Director of IT, in addition to being the Chairman and CEO of his own companies. Hunter has worked in many industries including insurance, healthcare, banking / financial services, education, consulting services, entertainment and military / defense at companies such as

General Electric, Wells Fargo Bank, Robert Half International and Blue Shield of California.

Hunter is also a social media pioneer as the founder of the first Internet-based global community started in 1994 called "The Park," with more than 700,000 members in 190 countries worldwide. He remains active on social media, with more than 500,000 Twitter followers.

Brent earned a B.S. in Math and Computer Science from Clarkson University, an M.S. in Counseling and Human Relations from Villanova University, and the equivalent of an M.S. in Information Systems after he graduated from the General Electric Company's fast-track Information Systems Management Program.

Brent is an Eagle Scout, a graduate of the U.S. Army Airborne School, and is involved with a number of global civic organizations, including a past position in the United Nations Association of the U.S. as the Vice President of Communications in the Northern California Division.

Hunter's first book, *The Pieces of Our Puzzle: An Integrated Approach to Personal Success and Well-Being,* provides a holistic synthesis of the world's major schools of psychology.

Another one of Brent's books is *The Rainbow Bridge: Bridge to Inner Peace and to World Peace,* which illuminates the common ground in the world's major wisdom traditions and includes a 14-Point Road Map to World Peace.

In addition, Hunter has compiled two books of quotes about wisdom, *Nuggets of Wisdom: Quotes to Ponder and Inspire* and *More Nuggets of Wisdom: Quotes to Ponder and Inspire,* and has written the upcoming *The Park Odyssey.*

After being born in Brooklyn, NY and living in Upstate New York, Philadelphia, Chicago and San Francisco, Brent currently lives, plays, and works in Los Angeles with his wife Dea, Golden Retriever Maisie and North American Sphynx Bindi.

CONTACT INFORMATION

Website: ThePowerofKM.com
Email: Brent@ThePowerofKM.com

INDEX

14-Point Road Map to
  World Peace 197
$1.5 billion 42, 54
$2 billion 16, 64
$5.3 trillion 111
$15 billion to $25 billion 55
$20.44 trillion 111
$30 billion 17
$50 billion 17
$85 million 16, 53
$90 trillion 17, 109
$200 million 16, 64
$500 million 16, 54

A

ABC123 Software 167, 174,
  191
Acuity Institute 42
ADKAR Change Manage-
  ment Model 128
after action review 50, 53
Agrarian Age 6

Albert Einstein 1, 117
American Red Cross 96
anesthesia 55, 149
anger 125, 126, 138, 142
apples 13, 14
Appreciative Inquiry 47
assessments 45, 46, 66, 120,
  169

B

Bank for International Settle-
  ments 111
Beckhard and Harris's
  Change Model 128
Ben and Jerry's 146
benchmarking 66
benefit corporation 145
Bernard of Chartres 149
best practices 53, 54
Best Practices 34, 53, 154,
  155
Big Picture 6

blogs 65
Blue Shield of California 196
BMW 144
BP Deepwater scandal 2
British Petroleum (BP) 16, 53
Brown Bag 43, 44, 81, 180
Buddy Program 36, 37, 77, 87, 162, 171, 176, 177, 178, 181, 190
bullying 39
Burke-Litwin's Change Model 128

C

call center 56
Cascade Engineering 146
centerforappreciativeinquiry. net 47
Change Curve 107
Change Management 72, 118, 122, 128, 133, 168, 190, 195
Change.org 146
Charles Savage 44
chat 65
checklist 53, 55
Chevron 16, 64
Chief Knowledge Officer 129
Chief Learning Officer 129
CKO 129, 130, 131

clean water 110
CLO 129
CNBC 2
CNET 2
CNN 2, 109
cnvc.org 48
common courtesy 138
common ground 136, 148, 197
common sense 18, 138
Communities of Action 62, 63
Communities of Interest 62, 63
communities of practice 112, 158, 165
communities of purpose 112, 165
Community of Action (CoA) 63
Community of Interest (CoI) 63
Community of Practice (CoP) 62
compassion 137, 147
conferencing 43, 65
conscious capitalism 143
continuous improvement 50
Continuous Improvement 154
Conversation, Dialogue and Diplomacy 157

corporate citizenship 143

corporate social responsibility (CSR) 143

creativity 14, 28, 61, 78, 79, 148, 179

Credit Suisse analysts 2

Crucial Conversations 47

Curiosity 1

D

dashboard 88, 89

David E. Hussey's EASIER Change Model 128

David Gurteen 44

Dea Hunter xv, 197

decorum 138

diamond 7, 21

DIKW Pyramid xvii, 12, 135, 136, 140

Director of Knowledge Management 130

DISC 46, 47, 78, 177

E

education xv, 111, 195

Edward Burnett Tylor 113

effectiveness 15, 17, 66, 70, 75, 77, 86, 87, 92, 94, 96, 115, 122, 154, 190

efficiency 2, 14, 15, 17, 50, 54, 64, 66, 75, 86, 92, 94, 96, 97, 111, 115, 122, 154, 190

Elisabeth Kübler-Ross 123, 125

Elizabeth Lank 44

employee retention 42

enigma machine 1

Enron scandal 2

Entovation International 44

Etsy 146

Eunika Mercier-Laurent 44

Everyday Democracy 97

Evox Television 146

exit interview 38, 39, 41, 82, 99

exit interviews 17, 29, 39, 42, 83, 171, 175, 176, 182, 183

expert directory 57

explicit knowledge 10, 11, 43, 50, 57, 62, 88, 132

extraordinary value of KM 9, 110, 111, 117, 160, 162, 164, 194

F

Farmigo 146

Food 98

Food and Agriculture Organization (FAO) 98

Forbes Magazine 144, 145

Ford Motor Company 16, 54

forums 65

Frank Leistner 15

frustration 127, 138

G

gaps 54, 83, 110, 182, 220
General Electric 196
GE's Change Acceleration Process (CAP) 128
global community 109, 112, 114, 196
Global Infrastructure Forum 109
globally-connected network of KM Communities 8, 112, 113, 114, 164, 165, 194
Google 144
Governance 118, 128, 168, 191

H

harmony 110, 160
Harvard 16, 55
Harvard School of Public Health 55
H.H. the 14th Dalai Lama xviii, 136
Hillel 137
Hogan Assessments 46
hoganassessments.com 46
Hootsuite 146
human capital 14, 15, 27, 86, 92, 94, 95, 151, 153, 160, 220

I

If We Only Knew What We Know 54
Industrial Age 6
Information Age 6, 7, 137, 153
information and communications technology (ICT) 113
Innovation 34, 44, 59, 60, 61, 78, 79, 148, 154, 175, 176, 179, 190
Innovation Award Program 60, 61, 78, 79
Innovation Awards 176, 179, 190
Innovation cafés 44
instant messaging 65
intellectual assets 14, 86
international currency trading 111
International Knowledge Management Institute ii, xv, 9, 53, 54, 64
International Labour Organization (ILO) 98
International Maritime Organization (IMO) 98
introspective 46, 50, 146
IT-centric 31, 69

K

Kenneth T. Derr 64
key phrases 26
keywords 26
Kickstarter 146
King Arthur Flour 146
Klean Kanteen 146
KM assessment 66
KM Champions Team 63
KM Champions Teams 62
KM Checkpoints 101
KM Communities i, 8, 63,
    94, 96, 107, 109, 112,
    113, 114, 157, 158, 164,
    165, 194
KM Community 63, 64, 78,
    94, 95, 101, 108, 112,
    114, 130, 162, 164, 171,
    177, 178, 179, 181, 192,
    194, 220
KM Council 130
KM dashboard 89
KM Leader 129, 130, 131,
    192
KM road map 185
knowing 5, 12, 140, 169
Knowledge Age 6, 7, 45,
    110, 137, 153, 159, 194
Knowledge Analyst 130
Knowledge Architect 130
Knowledge Base 56, 75, 173

knowledge café 44
Knowledge Champions Team
    63, 64, 78, 94, 95, 101,
    108, 112, 114, 130, 162,
    164, 177, 178, 179, 181,
    190, 192
Knowledge Council 130,
    131, 192
Knowledge Engineer 130
Knowledge Hierarchy 12
Knowledge Librarian 130
Knowledge Manager 4, 130
Knowledge Pyramid 12
knowledge repository 30,
    56, 57, 98, 171, 174, 180,
    181, 182, 183, 184
Knowledge Specialist 130
knowledge transfer 38, 75,
    77, 155, 173, 176
Know Thyself 146
Kotter's 8 Step Change
    Model 128
kryptonite 106, 220
Kübler-Ross Change Curve
    107
Kübler-Ross's Five Stages
    Model 128

L

law and order 111
layoffs 38
learning curve 36, 38

learning organization 38, 43

lessons learned 38, 50, 52, 53

lessons learned ground rules 38, 51

Lessons Learned Management Process (LLMP) 38, 52

Lessons Learned Management System 38

Lessons Learned Management System (LLMS) 52

Lessons Learned Meeting Ground Rules 38, 51

Lewin's Change Management Model 38

love 38

M

Mastering Organizational Knowledge Flow: How to Make Knowledge Sharing Work 15

McKinsey & Company 15, 57, 58

McKinsey's 7-S Model 15

Megatrends 15

Mentorship Program 15, 37

meta tags 15

method 44, 53, 109, 112, 115

Method 15

metrics 44, 53, 109, 112, 115

Miller's Law 44, 53, 109, 112, 115

More Nuggets of Wisdom 44, 53, 109, 112, 115, 197

More Nuggets of Wisdom: Quotes to Ponder and Inspire viii

Myers-Briggs Type Indicator (MBTI) 44, 46, 53, 109, 112, 115

N

Natura 44, 53, 109, 112, 115

New England Journal of Medicine 44, 53, 55, 109, 112, 115

non-linear 44, 53, 109, 112, 115

Nonviolent Communication (NVC) 44, 48, 53, 109, 112, 115

Nuggets of Wisdom 44, 53, 109, 112, 115, 197

Nuggets of Wisdom: Quotes to Ponder and Inspire viii

O

O'Dell and Grayson 44, 53, 54, 109, 112, 115

off-boarding 44, 53, 109, 112, 115

on-boarding 34, 42, 123

On Death and Dying 123

Operations Guide 123
Operations Manual 36, 123
Outward Bound 49, 123
outwardbound.org 49, 123

P

Patagonia 123
Personal Knowledge Management (PKM) 123
Peter M. Senge 43, 123
pilot 123
pity city 127
Play Book 36, 127
Plum Organics 127
Popeye 127
Positive deviance 48, 127
positivedeviance.org 48, 127
post mortem 50, 127
poverty 127
Primitive Culture 127
productivity 127
puzzle 127

R

rabbit holes 127
race relations 127
rainbow 127
Resource Guide 36, 146
retrospective 50, 146
Robert Half International 146, 196

ROI 146
romance 146
Royal Dutch Shell Group 146

S

Seven Key Facets of KM 146
Seven Key Lenses of KM 146
Seven Key Pillars of KM 146
Seven Key Practice Areas 146
Seven Step KM Strategy 146, 218, 219
Seventh Generation 146
shelter 110
Sir Francis Bacon 1, 106, 220
social bookmarking 106, 220
social networks 106, 220
social software 106, 220
Solberg Manufacturing 106, 220
spinach 106, 220
Stephen Covey's 7 Habits Model 1
Stephen Hawking 1
StrengthsFinder 45
strengthsfinder.com 45
Subject Matter Expert (SME) directory 57

succession plan 142

superhero 142

superpower 142

T

tacit knowledge 50, 57, 142

taxonomies 142

team-building 44, 48, 142

teamwork 142

Temet Nosce 142

terrorism 142

Texas Instruments 16, 54

The Brookings Institution 109

The Enneagram in Business 47

theenneagraminbusiness. com 47

The Fifth Discipline 43

the Golden Rule 137

the greatest issues of our time 112, 114

The Honest Company 146

The Knowledge-Creating Company xxiii

The Park 146, 196

The Park Odyssey 146, 197

The Pieces of Our Puzzle 146, 196

The Pieces of Our Puzzle: An Integrated Approach to Personal Success and Well-Being viii

the Platinum Rule 146

The Rainbow Bridge 146, 197

The Rainbow Bridge: Bridge to Inner Peace and to World Peace viii

The Temple of Apollo at Delphi 146

The World Café 44

Triodos Bank 146

trough of disillusionment 127

U

United Nations 98, 108, 110, 196

V

valley of despair 127

Virginia Satir's Change Process 128

vitalsmarts.com/crucialconversations 47

Volkswagen scandal 1

VP/SVP/EVP of Knowledge Management 130

W

Warby Parker 146

Welcome Packet 36, 74, 75

Wells Fargo Bank 196

Wikipedia xvii, 3, 44, 48, 125, 140, 145, 148

wikipedia.org 46

wikis 65

William Bridge's Transition
    Model 128

wisdom 38, 41, 52, 197

Wisdom viii, 7, 8, 12, 13,
    134, 135, 138, 153, 156,
    197

Wisdom Hierarchy 12

Wisdom-Infused Knowledge
    153

Wisdom Pyramid 12

World Food Programme
    (WFP) 98

World Health Organization
    (WHO) 55, 98

Y

yellow pages 57

yoga 105

NOTES TO MYSELF

As you read each chapter, jot down your questions, thoughts and ideas on these blank pages. The content of the book as well as your own notes will create a useful resource to help guide you on your journey through Knowledge Management.

Notes to Myself

(Seven Key Facets of KM)

Notes to Myself

(Seven Key Facets of KM)

Notes to Myself
(Seven Key Practice Areas of KM)

Notes to Myself

(Seven Key Practice Areas of KM)

Notes to Myself
(Seven Key Pillars of KM)

Notes to Myself
(Seven Key Pillars of KM)

Notes to Myself

(Seven Key Lenses of KM)

Notes to Myself
(Seven Key Lenses of KM)

Notes to Myself
(Seven Step KM Strategy)

Notes to Myself
(Seven Step KM Strategy)

Questions to Ask Ourselves (all KM Lenses)

What is our vision and mission?

Are we maximizing our human capital?

Are we maximizing our knowledge?

What are we doing to address our knowledge gaps?

Who am I / are we?

What do I / we stand for?

Why am I / are we here?

What is my / our purpose?

What am I / are we doing?

What am I / are we not doing?

What is my superpower?

What is my kryptonite?

What is my spinach?

Do I / we participate in a KM Community?

If not now, when?

Notes to Myself

Notes to Myself

Notes to Myself

Notes to Myself

Notes to Myself

Notes to Myself

Notes to Myself

Notes to Myself

Notes to Myself

Notes to Myself